SMALL GROUP
IDEA BOOK

Resources to Enrich

- community

- worship

- prayer

- study

- outreach

CINDY BUNCH, EDITOR

NOW WITH IDEAS FROM THE SMALL GROUP NETWORK

InterVarsity Press
Downers Grove, Illinois

InterVarsity Press
P.O. Box 1400, Downers Grove, IL 60515-1426
World Wide Web: www.ivpress.com
E-mail: mail@ivpress.com

InterVarsity Press® is the book-publishing division of InterVarsity Christian Fellowship/USA®, a student movement active on campus at hundreds of universities, colleges and schools of nursing in the United States of America, and a member movement of the International Fellowship of Evangelical Students. For information about local and regional activities, write Public Relations Dept., InterVarsity Christian Fellowship/USA, 6400 Schroeder Rd., P.O. Box 7895, Madison, WI 53707-7895, or visit the IVCF website at <www.ivcf.org>.

All Scripture quotations, unless otherwise indicated, are taken from the Holy Bible, New International Version®. NIV®. Copyright ©1973, 1978, 1984 by International Bible Society. Used by permission of Zondervan Publishing House. All rights reserved.

A list of entries used with the permission of the Small Group Network is found on page 187.

Cover design: Cindy Kiple

Cover and interior image: Neo Vision/Photonica

ISBN 0-8308-1124-9

Printed in the United States of America ∞

Library of Congress Cataloging-in-Publication Data

Small group idea book: resources to enrich community, worship,
prayer, study, outreach/Cindy Bunch, editor,—Rev. and
expanded ed.
    p. cm.
Includes bibliographical references.
    ISBN 0-8308-1124-9 (pbk.: alk. paper)
    1. Church group work. 2. Small groups—Religious
aspects—Christianity. I. Bunch, Cindy.
    BV652.2.S57 2003
253'.7—dc22
                                                    2003018904

P	19	18	17	16	15	14	13	12	11	10	9	8	7	6	5	4	3	2	1
Y	19	18	17	16	15	14	13	12	11	10	09	08	07	06	05	04	03

CONTENTS

In 1982 a small group of InterVarsity Christian Fellowship (IVCF) staff-workers (Steve Barker, Judy Johnson, Jimmy Long, Rob Malone and Ron Nicholas, who coordinated their work) created *The Small Group Leader's Handbook*. Used by a variety of groups, including prison ministries and Officer's Christian Fellowship, that groundbreaking book was of great service to both the campus and the church.

In 1995 another team (Jimmy Long [the group's coordinator], Ann Beyerlein, Sara Keiper, Patty Pell, Nina Thiel and Doug Whallon) wrote a new handbook called *The Small Group Leader's Handbook: The Next Generation*, which I edited. In the process of writing that book we found that one of the most valued features of the original book was the resource section. We decided that there was enough helpful material available to create a separate book of resources. Thus the *Small Group Idea Book* was born.

The book is a collaborative effort. We included ideas from small group specialists as well as InterVarsity staff and students from across the country. We particularly want to thank the Downstate Illinois team, who submitted the most ideas of any IVCF area and won a pizza party. Runners-up included Central/South New Jersey and Western Washington. Many ideas from the original resource section of *The Small Group Leader's Handbook*, compiled by Judy Johnson, are here as well.

The material made its debut on the InterVarsity Press website in the Small Group Idea Center, and readers were invited to contribute their ideas. This expanded edition includes ideas that we have gathered from the Web. We have also included ideas and an appendix from Dan Lentz and Michael Mack and their Small Group Network <www.SmallGroups.com>.

There are four sections which represent the four key components of a small group: community, worship and prayer, Bible study and outreach.

Ideas within each section are organized alphabetically. Using a mix of ideas from each of these four sections will help group members to grow in their relationship with God and one another.

Some of the sections are subdivided to make them more useful. In chapter one, "Community Resources," we have provided ideas that are appropriate for any phase of a group's life. You'll find ideas for the first few meetings of a small group, ideas for the start-up phase as people continue to question what the group is and whether they want to be a part of it, ideas for the shake-up or conflict phase when the honeymoon is over and group ownership is established, ideas for the live-it-up or action phase when real community is taking place and people are growing, and ideas for the wrap-up phase when the group disbands and needs celebration and closure. Outreach is divided into five key areas: getting started, serving others, reaching seekers, world mission and social action.

We plan to expand and update this book as needed, so if you have ideas you would like to submit for a future edition, feel free to send them to me at InterVarsity Press, P.O. Box 1400, Downers Grove, IL 60515. I can be reached via email at smallgroups@ivpress.com. (By submitting an idea you are granting InterVarsity Press permission to reprint your idea. If we use your idea and have a correct mailing address, we will send you a copy of the new edition.) You may also be interested in our small group resources located on the InterVarsity Press website. Visit there to send me your ideas or feedback on the book.

Small groups are a powerful way for people to connect with one another and experience the power of the gospel. May God bless your small group ministry.

Cindy Bunch

PART ONE

COMMUNITY

To help make this chapter useful we've divided it into five sections: ideas for any phase of group life, and then ideas for the four typical phases of small group life: start-up, shake-up (the stage of conflict and commitment), live-it-up (the action stage once a group has gelled) and wrap-up (the period of bringing a group to a close). Some sections are also subdivided by the length of time the activities require. This should help you find the ideas that fit your needs.

ACTIVITIES FOR ANY PHASE OF A GROUP'S LIFE

These ideas are designed to help you "check in" with each other about how you're doing, encourage each other and enjoy being together.

AFFIRMATION EXERCISE

Ann Beyerlein

Write each person's name on the top of a sheet of paper. Pass the pages around the group and write words of affirmation and encouragement on each person's page. Use these pages to thank God for each other.

E-MAIL ENCOURAGEMENT

Amy Brooke

Breaks the group up into partners who will e-mail each other regularly to challenge one another to keep up with quiet times and Bible study. Talk about what God is teaching you between small groups or as you reflect on the small group meeting.

FOUND COLLAGE

Irma Hider

Give each member five minutes to go outside and collect garbage. It must consist of things that aren't useful anymore—a dead flower, rocks, bottle caps, paper bags, flyers; they can't buy anything. If the activity is being done at a first, second or third meeting, have members make something that describes themselves using all of the garbage they collected. If the activity is part of a closing meeting, have each member pick someone else's name out of a hat and make something that reflects the other person—something they appreciated about them or something they see them doing in the future. Another variation, instead of going out and looking for garbage, is to have the leader bring miscellaneous materials such as Q-Tips, cotton balls, construction paper, paper plates, crayons, tacks, Popsicle sticks, bottle caps, Pringles cans, balloons, paper cups or paper clips.

INFORMAL GATHERINGS
University of Illinois campus staff

Spending time together in informal settings will help group members become more comfortable with each other and help them appreciate people in different environments. Some possibilities are to

- go out to eat together
- make popcorn, ice cream or pizza
- play volleyball, football, softball or soccer
- make a meal together or have a cookout
- plan a retreat in which you can incorporate many activities
- read a fun story such as *Winnie the Pooh, The Velveteen Rabbit* or a book by Dr. Seuss
- play board games like the Ungame, Scattergories, Cranium or Trivial Pursuit
- read a play aloud together, each taking a different role; there are many good ones in *A Man Born to Be King* (It's good nurture too!)
- go on a hike, or go fly a kite
- do laundry together
- watch a movie
- go ice skating, rollerblading or bowling
- visit each other's churches
- greet people at large group or at church on Sunday morning
- go on a road trip to visit an inner-city ministry
- do something with another small group (challenge them to a volleyball game, Pictionary tournament, etc.)
- go as a group to see members who are on a sports team, in the choir or in a play

POSTCARDS FROM HOME

Amy Brooke

This activity is good to do before a break in your meetings for holidays or the summer. On three-by-five "postcards," have each person write to the group about their ideal break. Mix them up and let people read someone else's to the group. Use this as a launching point to talk about expectations and concerns prior to break.

PURCHASING PAIRS

Irma Hider

This is a good activity to help prayer partners get to know each other. The leader gives each pair one or two dollars to spend. They are to buy something for the whole group and bring it to the next meeting. When done early in the year, it encourages people to return to small group to report. If done later in the year, when group members know each other, have the pairs buy things that are characteristic of certain members. For example, Carrie gets a Band-Aid because she is great at helping others. Mark gets chocolate with almonds because he is sweet and nutty. Members get to know each other by what they bring.

ROUNDS

A round is when each member of the group is given thirty seconds at the beginning or the end of any group session. It is designed to be a short status report. No feedback or evaluation of one another is allowed. After everyone has shared, the group has the option of following up or asking clarification of a group member. A short, quick round may do several things for a group:

- Members become more aware of their feelings.

- They learn to report feelings (emotions) without evaluation.

- Hidden agendas that may otherwise hinder the group process may be brought out into the open, or unfinished business at the end of a meeting may be discovered.

- Openness and freedom to share may become a natural part of group experience.

- The exercise can help in transition when people may need encouragement to share.

The round can be adapted by having everyone report their feelings in weather terminology—partly cloudy, sunny and so on. This can often be more helpful for people who have trouble using feeling words.

SCAVENGER HUNT

Jane Jung

This activity is intended as a competition among several small groups within a church or fellowship. It promotes small groups among your fellowship and encourages bonding among small group members.

Each group takes a disposable camera to photograph various scenes or situations in their area. An identical list is given to each group and may include such photographs as the whole group eating the same food (such as ice cream cones or lollipops), or the whole group in one car or in front of an ethnic restaurant. The group that photographs the most scenarios on the list is the winner. Afterward, each group develops its photographs and hangs them up for everyone in the fellowship to see.

THE SPIRITUAL ATHLETE

L. Choi and M. Wang

Having group members take an assessment of their spiritual health (revealing as much detail as they wish) gives the small group leader a clue as to how to minister to the group. (See the figure on p. 15.)

SPIRITUAL SCULPTING

Christopher Shaw

Distribute several cans of kids' Play Dough to members of the group. Give each person ten minutes to make something out of the Play Dough (figure, object, sculpture) that represents "who they are" spiritually at that time.

Check All Symptoms That Apply

___ Sore Achilles Heel (a perpetual sin)

___ Headaches

___ Healthy

___ Heartaches

___ Hungry for meat

___ Lame-footed

___ In need of a coach

___ In need of encouragement

___ Overanxious

___ Off the path

___ On crutches

___ Overfed and underexercised

___ Starving

___ Tendinitis

___ Tunnel vision

___ Underchallenged

___ Weary

What Type of Runner Are You?

___ Loner

___ Pack runner (need constant support to stay on track)

___ Running in circles (lacking vision)

___ Sprinter (strong for a while; need to grow in endurance)

___ Strong and even-paced (steadily making progress; welcomes challenges)

Where Are You on the Road of the Saints?

___ Waiting to start

___ Newborn

___ Toddler

___ Adolescent (Growing Pains)

___ Young adult

___ Mentor

What I want to accomplish by the end of the year:

Needs I have right now:

Then give everyone two to three minutes to describe what they made and why.

This is an extremely effective visual tool. People remember the "silly objects" other group members made, and they are reminded of how they can pray for that each other during the week.

IDEAS FOR THE FIRST FEW MEETINGS

These are get-acquainted games and discussions to help you break the ice. Many are brief, so you may want to use several. Some of these ideas are active and may seem silly to group members, but acting goofy can help people feel more relaxed. These ideas will be helpful to you for the first three to six meetings; after that you'll want to move on to activities that will take you deeper.

APPOINTMENTS
Tom Sirinides

Hand out sheets of paper. Draw lines to make four sections. Number the areas one through four.. Now make appointments with four different people. Once everyone has four different people's names written down, the leader calls, "Number one!" and everyone gets together with the first appointment. Introduce yourselves and ask each other about your day or week. In a little while, the leader calls, "Number two!" and so on until all the appointments have been completed. You can have people set up more than or fewer than four appointments depending on the time available. Allow five to ten minutes per appointment.

BAG SKITS
Tom Sirinides

Before people arrive, get two or three shopping bags, one bag for every team you'll have. Put five to ten random items from around your home (or dorm room) in each bag. The things in each bag should be different from those in the others. It doesn't matter what items you choose; be creative or dull. When people arrive, divide into teams, one team for each bag you have.

Give each group a bag. They have ten minutes (or some such time) to create a skit using all the objects in their bag and every person in their group.

BE AN OREO
Priscilla Luming

Buy a bag of Oreo cookies. Go around the circle and tell and demonstrate how you go about eating an Oreo. Then share how your style of eating it reflects your personality. For example, "I take the cookie apart, making sure the inside cream is intact and the outside cookies are clean. I eat the inside first, then the cookie parts. This shows that I am particular about how things are done, chronologically and orderly."

THE COMMONS GAME
Dave Suryk

Go around the circle and spend five minutes seeing how many somewhat interesting things everyone has in common (all are left-handed, no one ever wore braces and so on). Things like "we have feet" don't count.

FICTIONARY
University of Illinois staff

One member of the group finds a word in the dictionary that they think nobody knows and reads the word to the group. While that person writes the real definition down on a sheet of paper, the other members make up definitions for the word, write them down and hand them in. The first member reads through the definitions, and people vote on which definition they think is the real one. One point is given to each person who guessed the right definition, and one point to the person whose made-up definition received the most votes. The game continues until all members have had a chance to find a word.

FORMING GROUPS
Tom Sirinides

This is a way to form random groups for a game or activity. Take one shoe from everyone, mix them up in a pile, and divide the pile into the number of groups you want. People look for their shoes and thus find their groups.

GIMME GIMME

Tom Sirinides

Divide into two or more teams and one leader (who is not on any team). The leader stands at the front of the room and says "Gimme gimme . . ." (as in "Give me, give me . . .") and then mentions something. Each team then races to give the leader that thing; the first team to do so gets a point. The leader should be creative in what he or she asks for—a certain type of shoe-lace, a Bible verse, a song sung (maybe in a language other than English!) or some sort of exercise or action.

GOOFY BOWLING

Sue Sage

Each member needs to bring five dollars and a good sense of humor to this event. Pair up and go to any thrift store. Each member "trusts" the other member of their pair to dress them for five dollars or less. Then go bowling as a group in your get-ups. Be sure to bring a camera, because this is great material for an end-of-the-year slide show.

HAND STOMP

Allen Lincoln

Everyone kneels forward on their hands in a circle. Each person puts their left hand to the left of the person's hand on their left—thus each person has someone else's hand between his or her own hands.

The game begins with someone "stomping" their hand on the ground. Going counterclockwise, the next hand stomps, moving around the circle. One stomp continues the direction. Two stomps reverse the direction. A hand is "taken out of the game" if it stomps out of order.

The game can get fast and furious with both hands involved in the game and reversals possible at any time! It ends when only one person is left, or two people agree to a tie.

KNOTS
University of Illinois staff

Everyone puts their hands into the middle of the circle and takes the hands of two others (not next to them). Try to untangle yourselves.

NAME THAT FACE
Tom Sirinides

Split into two groups. Have a blanket held up between the two groups so that they can't see each other. Each team positions one person facing the center of the blanket. On the count of three, the blanket is dropped, and the two people are suddenly facing each other. The first one to call out the other's name "wins." Repeat the process. (It's one way to learn names!)

THE NO-GIFT GAME
Sue Sage

This is a great Christmastime game. You need one pair of dice and two wrapped gifts for every ten people who are at the party. The gifts are best if they are inexpensive and of the white elephant variety. Everyone sits in a circle with the gifts in the middle. Give people the pairs of dice. Set a timer for five minutes and let the fun begin.

Each person rolls the dice hoping for doubles. When someone gets doubles they run to the middle and get a gift out of the center. (Roll the dice only once, and then pass them on.) When there are no gifts left in the center, you can take a gift from someone else. At the end of five minutes whoever has the gifts can keep them and must unwrap their treasure so that everyone can see what the ruckus was all about.

QUIZ GAME
Bill Fader

Have each person in the group tell their name, hometown, major or occupation, number of siblings, favorite subject in school and any other tidbits of information you'd like to include. Then people divide into two groups. The small group leader will call out the name of a person and an info tidbit

("What is Sally's favorite subject?"). The other team has time to confer (three seconds) and give the answer. Score is kept.

This game could also be done in pairs with partners reporting back to the group to give each other's personal history.

SCREAMING VIKINGS
Henry Lee

Screaming Vikings is a hysterically funny game well suited to a group in the early stages or to an established group that needs a break for hilarity. You probably need twenty to thirty minutes to play.

Group members need to sit in a circle in chairs or on the floor.

Round One

The leader of the game is It. He or she points at someone and says, "Bipity, bipity, bop." If the other person says "Bop" before the leader is finished, the leader points to another person. If the other person doesn't say "Bop" in time, then he or she becomes It, and the first person sits down. The person who is It can alternate saying "Bipity, bipity, bop" with saying just "Bop." The proper response to "Bop" is nothing. If the person pointed at says "Bop," then he or she becomes It.

Round Two

The leader may alternate the above with the command "squirrel." Whoever is pointed at must then put their hands up to their face like paws and put their teeth over their lower lip. The people on either side of the person (even if there is an empty chair) make the eyes of the squirrel by forming a circle with the thumb and forefinger and placing one eye over each side of the squirrel's face. If any part of the squirrel is not formed correctly by the time the leader counts to ten, that person is It.

Round Three

A further level of complexity is created when the first two commands are alternated with "screaming vikings." The person the leader points to puts their hands on top of their head to form antlers. The people on either side row the boat with their hands going in the correct direction. All three people scream. Anyone not doing the proper thing by the time the leader counts to ten becomes It.

Round Four

If the leader gives the command "elephant," the person pointed to makes an elephant trunk with one arm wrapped around the other. The people on either side form ears on the elephant with their arms formed in a *C* shape.

SIGNIFICANT CLOTHING

Priscilla Luming

Have people sit in a circle and share the significance of an item of clothing (or anything they're wearing—a watch, jewelry) that tells about themselves.

STORYTELLING

Bill Fader

The small group leader gives a list of approximately eight words to the members, who are working in pairs. Each pair works together to develop a story using those words and then presents their story to the group.

SURPRISE GUEST

Tom Sirinides

Each person puts their name on a slip of paper. Drop these in a hat and let each person draw one out. Don't tell whose name you drew, but during the next week, you must visit that person. If you see them without trying to do so (for example, in the dining hall or at the store), you fulfill your "obligation" only if you actually talk with them for thirty minutes or more.

A variation on this is to eliminate the surprise and just have people set up meal or other appointments right then and there for the week ahead.

TWO TRUTHS AND A LIE

Tell two things about yourself that are true and one that is a lie. Everyone tries to guess which one is not true.

IDEAS FOR START-UP

These ideas are for groups in the early phase of life. The start-up or exploration phase is the honeymoon period for groups. Some of these may work for you during the shake-up or conflict phase as well.

BEAUTIFUL BABIES
Priscilla Luming

Make "baseball cards" out of baby pictures of people in your small group. Each person writes important facts on them such as birthplace, your full name, what your name would have been if you had been born the other sex. Enjoy passing them around to one another. (This activity takes less than fifteen minutes.)

BEST FRIEND
Tom Sirinides

Ask each person to describe their best friend. (A variation is for them to describe their favorite family member. This activity takes less than fifteen minutes.)

BRUSH WITH GREATNESS
Kurt Paulsen

This idea was inspired by *The Late Show with David Letterman*. Each person is given a small sheet of paper. They are to write on it an experience they have had with a famous (or semi-famous or infamous!) person. This can range from simply seeing someone famous at the same restaurant to actually meeting someone famous.

After everyone is finished, scramble the papers and pass them out so that no person gets their own paper. Each person is then to "finish" the story by means of a "writer's embellishment" (they can make up whatever they want as a way to end the story).

The leader then reads each of the stories with the writer's embellishment. The group tries to guess who wrote the original story and who wrote the writer's embellishment.

The purpose of this activity is to find out something unusual about each person in a nonthreatening way. It is also a source of laughter and a good discussion starter.

This can also be used to introduce a Bible study on the Gospels or Acts. For example, if you are studying early Gospel chapters, move from this activity to looking at how people react to Jesus, a "famous person" of his day in the passage. (This activity takes less than thirty minutes.)

CHILDHOOD FAVORITES
Irma Hider

Have each person bring something they ate while growing up. You can do this as a dinner potluck or as a snack or study break. While eating, talk about what you brought. It's great for talking about people's backgrounds. (This activity takes less than thirty minutes.)

COAT OF ARMS

A coat of arms in the past used signs and symbols to tell something about a person or family (see the figure on p. 24). Make your own coat of arms, describing things about yourself. Write your answers in the appropriate spaces, or for those creative people, feel free to draw.

- Upper left: Two things you do well.

- Middle left: Your greatest success in life.

- Lower left: What you would do with one year left to live.

- Upper right: "Psychological home" or place where you feel most at home.

- Middle right: Three people most influential in your life or who mean the most to you.

- Lower right: Three words you would like said about you.

Talk about your coat of arms with the group. (This activity takes less than thirty minutes.)

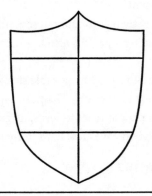

A coat of arms

Alternate questions by InterVarsity staff at the University of Illinois:

- What animal represents you best?
- If time or money were not barriers, what is the job that you would like to do most in the future?
- What kind of home would you like to live in?
- Who is the person who has had the most influence on your life?
- What do you like to look at the most?

COLLAGES

Using magazine pictures and words, have each member make a collage that describes something about themselves. If you are outside, you could gather natural materials (shells, cones, plants, sand and so on) to make the collage. (This activity takes less than thirty minutes.)

COMING AND GOING

Kent E. Fillinger

Purchase mailing labels with the "From" and the "To" sections marked. Each group member gets one label and writes in the "From" section where they are from originally (where they were born or grew up). Then in the

"To" section they write where they would want to go if they could go "to" anywhere in the world.

After everyone has shared their answers with the group, the next level of community building can take place. The leader instructs each person to write in the "From" section where they are coming "from" spiritually (spiritual background/history) and in the "To" section where they would like to get "to" spiritually as a result of participating in the group.

A final option is to take the "To" answers and talk about the goals or objectives for the group and even a format for a group covenant.

This activity provides multiple levels of discussion and can be adapted to meet the needs of the group. (This activity takes less than fifteen minutes.)

COMMUNITY CRAPS
Shawn Young

Bring a pair of dice and take turns rolling. According to the numbers you roll, do or answer the following (this activity takes less than fifteen minutes):

2   What movie/TV character are you most like?

3   The person three places to the left may ask you two questions.

4   What do people of the opposite sex like about you?

5   Who has been the biggest influence on you?

6   Ask a question of anyone you choose.

7   What was the best moment of your life?

8   What three words would you use to describe God?

9   Sing at least nine words of your favorite song.

10   Finish this sentence: "I hate it when . . . "

11   Of all the people in the room, who do you have the least in common with? Treat that person to lunch this week. (Make an appointment with them before you leave today.)

12   Do all the stupid-human tricks you know.

DIAGRAMS

Think about who you are. What terms would you use to describe yourself? On a plain sheet of paper diagram some aspects of your personality by using small pictures. Don't worry about your artistic ability. Pair off within the group, and explain your diagram to your partner. Have your partner ask you questions about your diagram until there is a good understanding of what you are trying to communicate. Now have your partner explain his or her diagram. After the group regathers, each person should explain to the group the diagram his or her partner drew. Take time to discuss what you have learned about each other and yourself. (This activity takes less than thirty minutes.)

DINNER TIME

University of Illinois staff

Describe dinner at your home—where people sat, whether your family ate together, who did the talking, what the topics were and so on. You may want to use crayons or markers to draw the table and family to use in your description. (This activity takes less than thirty minutes.)

DO YOU BELIEVE?

University of Illinois staff

Give everyone ten pennies. Let each person have a chance to say something they have done that they don't believe anyone else has done. Everyone who has done it before must give that person a penny. The game continues until someone runs out of pennies. M&Ms can be used in place of pennies. (This activity takes less than fifteen minutes.)

DRAW YOUR HOPE

Allen Lincoln

This exercise will help you evaluate your spiritual growth and see how God is working. In a small group meeting early in the year have everyone draw a plant. At the bottom, they should write in what they hope to be rooted in during the semester or set period of time (the world, Christian relationships, Christ's principles, prayer and so on). For the stem/trunk, they should label how they will live that out (being part of a small group, attending church and fellowship meetings, working through a Christian book, regular quiet times). For the leaves, branches, flowers, they should write all the things they hope to have grown as fruit in their lives by the end of the given time (Scripture is alive to them, led someone to Christ, more at peace every day, overcome an addiction or sin). Allow people to talk about their trees with one another at a level they feel comfortable with; you might want to divide into pairs for this.

Then put the drawings away until the end of set period of time. At the last meeting, pull them out again and see how your tree did. Talk about what came true, what didn't and why. What unexpected growths took place? Any sudden tree diseases hit? Offer prayers of thanksgiving for what God did during the semester. (This activity takes less than an hour.)

DREAMING
Stephanie Moser

If there were no limits on time, talent or training, no obstacles in the way, what would you do for God? (This activity takes less than fifteen minutes.)

FILL IN THE BLANK (SORT OF)
Scott Hotaling

Everyone thinks of a way to fill in the sentence "I used to _____, but now I just _____." Then, one person begins and completes the first half of the sentence, and the next person completes the second half in the way he or she had planned. The second person then says the first part of the sentence and the third person finishes it. This continues until each person contributes. (This activity takes less than fifteen minutes.)

THE FRIENDSHIP FACTOR
Nairy Ohanian

This activity explores attributes of friendships and helps members share their history of friends. Leaders bring white paper and crayons. Take a few minutes to have each member draw a picture of their closest friend. This does not need to be artistic; just have fun. Include features that are unique to him or her. Then write two characteristics you appreciate most about this friend. Discuss the pictures and the characteristics of good friendships. Notice the traits that other members really desire in friends and work at nurturing those qualities in the group. (This activity takes less than fifteen minutes.)

GUESS WHO?

Tom Sirinides

Everyone writes a sentence about themselves, then crumples their paper up and throws it into the middle of the circle. Each person then picks one up. One person opens theirs and reads it. The group then tries to decide whose it might be. Even the person whose it actually is can participate in the discussion; don't lie, but don't give yourself away either. Continue one by one until all the papers are opened. An added challenge is to wait to reveal the true answers until all have been opened and assigned. The group may want to change some previous guesses as the new papers are opened up. (This activity takes less than fifteen minutes.)

HEROES

Tom Sirinides

Ask, "Who was your hero as a child?" Or, "Who was your favorite TV character as a child?" Or ask about favorite cartoon characters. (This activity takes less than fifteen minutes.)

HOUSE ON FIRE

Tom Sirinides

Read the following scenario:

1. Your home is on fire. Everyone is safely outside and you have about one minute to run through the place to collect three or four things you would want to save. Write those things down.

2. Now tell us the items on your list and also why you chose each one.

3. What have you learned about the things that you value?

This activity takes less than thirty minutes.

"I DIDN'T KNOW THAT"
Dave Ivaska

Tell the group something about yourself that they'd never think to ask you about. (This activity takes less than fifteen minutes.)

IMPACT
Tom Sirinides

Ask each person to tell about someone who has had a significant impact on his or her life (for good, for bad, in whatever area they choose). (This activity takes less than fifteen minutes.)

I'VE NEVER
Tom Sirinides

Give each person ten beans (or ten pennies, or just have them hold up their ten fingers!). The first player makes a statement like "I've never seen the ocean," or "I've never left the United States." (It must be a true statement.) Any player who has done that thing (that is, seen the ocean, left the United States) loses one bean or penny or puts down one finger. Continue around the circle until only one person has any beans, pennies or raised fingers left. (This activity takes less than fifteen minutes.)

JUST SAVE ONE
Tom Sirinides

Pass around a bowl of colored candies (M&Ms, Reese's Pieces, Skittles). Tell people to eat as many as they want but to save one piece. After everyone has only one piece, announce a "question to answer" for each color. For example:

Red: Tell about a happy day in your life.

Green: Tell someplace you'd like to visit and why.

Yellow: Talk about someone you'd like to meet, and why.

Orange: List three traits you'd like in a spouse.

Brown: Share about a movie you enjoyed and why.

This activity takes less than fifteen minutes.

LET'S CELEBRATE!
Nairy Ohanian

This activity allows internationals to reconnect with home and exposes group members to each other's cultural traditions. Each person should describe their favorite spiritual or cultural holiday, its purpose, how it is celebrated, how their family celebrates it and why it is their favorite. Try to connect each holiday to a similar U.S. holiday or tradition. Allow members to ask questions of each other. (This activity takes less than fifteen minutes.)

LIFELINE
Thinking back as far as you can, draw a graph that represents your life. Consider the high points, the low points, moments of inspiration, moments of despair, leveling-off times and where you are now. The line will probably be a mixture of straight, slanted, jagged, curved lines. After you've drawn it, share what it means to you with others in your group. (This activity takes less than an hour.)

MORE THAN A WORD
Tom Sirinides

Each person answers the question: "When, if ever, did God become more than a word to you?" (This activity takes less than fifteen minutes.)

MOVIE MAKING
Sue Sage

This works if you have a couple of VCRs and a camcorder available, plus a couple of technology buffs to do the editing. This usually takes an entire evening and is at its best when it gets really late. The basic gist is to find a crazy idea and film a movie out of it. Titles have included *Star Trek: The Lost Generation*, *The Forgiven* (a western with a happy ending) and *Clueless* (a mystery).

MY LIFE'S A PIPE CLEANER
Tom Sirinides

Hand out pipe cleaners. Each person bends theirs to tell something about their break, their week, how they are feeling right now, and so on. (Think up your own ideas; this activity takes less than fifteen minutes.)

ONE DAY
Tom Sirinides

Each person answers the question, "If you could relive one day of your life, which day would it be?" Or "If you could have one day off unexpectedly, how would you spend it?" (This activity takes less than fifteen minutes.)

PENNY PASS
University of Illinois staff

Give a penny to a group member. All of the group members bombard that person with his or her strengths or gifts. After a few minutes they pass the penny to the next person. (This activity takes less than thirty minutes.)

PICTURE THIS
Tiffany Stack

Cut out a variety of pictures from magazines, catalogs or newspapers. Lay them in the center of the group, and ask members to choose three pictures to describe themselves. Then have people tell the group how the pictures describe them. (This activity takes less than fifteen minutes.)

POCKETS
Tom Sirinides

Each person shows the group (and talks about) three things from their pockets, wallet, backpack or purse that tell something about them. (This activity takes less than fifteen minutes.)

PROVERBS
Tom Sirinides

If your group includes internationals, have everyone share a proverb from his or her home country. (This activity takes five to fifteen minutes.)

REVELATIONS
Cal Stevens

"Revelations" is a game for small groups who want to go deeper. Your group may compete against other small groups or against each other. When playing against other small groups, the object of the game is to have your team members reach fifty points as close to the same time as possible. When playing against other members of your small group, the object is to reach fifty points—without going over fifty—first. (This activity takes less than an hour.)

Photocopy a personal inventory (below) for each player. You also need one die and a deck of regular playing cards.

Complete the following statements, and then rate them according to how difficult they are to complete. Give the one you find easiest to complete a 1, the one most difficult a 10.

_____ The dumbest thing I ever did was _____

_____ The best thing about me is _____

_____ One thing I'll do differently from my parents is _____

_____ One thing I'd like to change about myself is _____

_____ This depresses me: _____

_____ I wish I could _____

_____ Family is _____

_____ My friends consider me _____

_____ I experienced love when _____

_____ My favorite music artist/group is _____ because _____

The personal inventory. Permission granted to photocopy this page for small group use. Taken from *Small Group Idea Book*, Cindy Bunch, ed., rev. ed. © 2003 by InterVarsity Press.

1. Instruct each group member to rank the personal inventory statements from 1 to 10, giving a 1 to the statement they find easiest to complete and a 10 to the one they find the most difficult.

2. Ask people to choose a token that means something special to them (a ring, for example, or a key) and share its significance with the group.

3. The oldest person begins by placing their token on *start*, rolling a die and moving the corresponding number of spaces. After they've taken the action indicated on the space where they land, play passes to the left. Keep answers to two minutes. (The playing board is found on page 35.)

4. Follow instructions on the playing board as follows:

- *Revelation:* Players draw a card and answer the item on their personal inventory which corresponds to the number on that card. They then receive that number of points. (A two of any suit means "give your two-point answer"; a three means "give your three-point answer"; and so on. Aces serve as one-point answer cards. Ignore or pull out jacks, queens and kings.) When someone draws a card for a question they have already answered, they must draw again. If they have answered all ten questions on their personal inventory, they may answer them a second time—differently, of course—for double points.

- *Retell Revelation:* Retell the last personal inventory answer given by someone else for five points.

- *Names:* Players receive one point for each person whose first, middle and last names they can remember. Players can only get points for recalling names once; those who land on the "Names" square a second time must roll again.

- *Truth Right (Left):* The person on the player's right or left can ask him or her anything not on the personal inventory. The player receives five points for answering.

- *Retell Truth:* Repeat the last truth shared by another person for five points.

- *History*: Give a two-minute personal history for five points. If you land on "History" a second time, share a different part of your life for ten points.

- *Retell History*: Recap the last personal history given by another person in the group for five points.

- *Observe High (Low)*: The player observes a quality in the person who has the highest (lowest) score—even if that's the player—for five points.

- *Inhibited!* No points this turn.

5. When playing against other groups, one person can pass a personal inventory question off to a teammate to help group members' scores stay on an even par.

   When playing against other members of the small group, one person can pass a personal inventory question off to someone else to keep from going over fifty points—as long as that question does not push the other person's score over fifty points.

   In either case, the person who receives the question gets the same number of points that the original player would have received. If the person to whom the question is passed has answered it before, they must answer it again, differently, for double points. Each player can pass off questions no more than three times.

6. If playing on teams, group members determine how many points away from fifty they are when someone on their team ends their group's playing time by scoring fifty or more points; this value is totaled and divided by the number of players to figure the average deviation. The group with the lowest average deviation from fifty wins. (Other small groups do not have to be present for you to compete against them. In fact, you may want to set up a small group "tournament" in which each group plays the game during a particular week early in the semester, then reports their average deviation score at the next large group meeting.)

7. When playing against other members of your small group, the game ends when someone hits exactly fifty points and wins, or goes over fifty points and loses. If no one scores exactly fifty points, the person with the score closest to fifty wins.

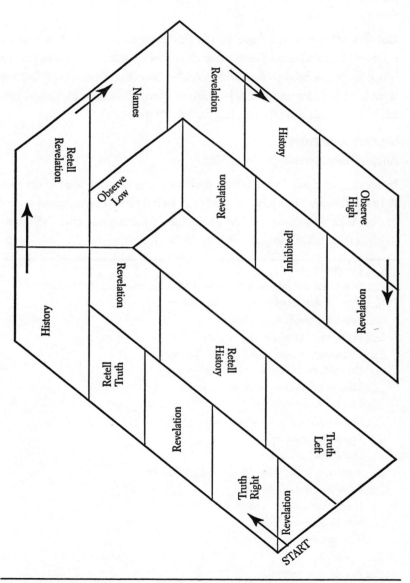

Revelations game board. Permission granted to photocopy this page for small group use. Taken from *Small Group Idea Book*, Cindy Bunch, ed., rev. ed. © 2003 by InterVarsity Press.

ROLES

Stephanie Moser

List five roles that you have in life (for example, a student, a sister, a mother). Then add an adjective that describes what kind of person you are (for example, a busy student) and another adjective describing what you want to be like (for example, a learning student). Take time to explain your adjectives. (This activity takes less than thirty minutes.)

SILENT AUCTION

Adapted from Serendipity *by Al Hsu*

In silence, jot down in the left margin the dollar amount you bid on each item listed below. The total amount you can bid for all items cannot exceed $1,000. When you open the bids, write the winner's name after each item. (This activity takes less than fifteen minutes.)

___ Pay off all loans

___ New personal computer, with printer, DVD player and unlimited Internet access

___ Season tickets for sports team of your choice

___ Lunch with the U.S. President

___ Internship at a Fortune 500 company

___ Opportunity to participate in the next Olympics

___ Date with the person of your dreams

___ Lifetime tickets to Broadway musicals

___ Role in a motion picture

___ Complete health insurance coverage

___ Trip around the world

___ Year of study in Europe

___ Acceptance to med school/law school/grad school

___ Down payment on a house

___ Happy marriage and/or family life

___ Recording contract

___ Term in Congress

___ A new job

___ Be a guest on Letterman

SNAPSHOTS
Sara Keiper

An alternate way to approach the coat-of-arms exercise, especially for those who aren't familiar with or comfortable with the idea of a coat of arms is to ask people to create a "photo album." Each photo describes in words or pictures something about different parts of your life. Categories could include something about your family, three words you'd like to have said about you, where you grew up, a place you dream of visiting, three people who have influenced you the most, where you feel most at home and your favorite dessert. (This activity takes less than thirty minutes.)

SQUARES
Priscilla Luming

Pass a roll of toilet paper around the group and tell each member to take as much toilet paper "as they think they need." For each square of paper they take, they must tell a joke, an embarrassing moment or a strange habit. (This activity takes less than fifteen minutes.)

THREE WORDS
Tom Sirinides

Each person answers one or more of the following questions (this activity takes less than fifteen minutes):

1. If you had to describe yourself in three words, what would they be?
2. If you had to describe your family in three words, what would they be?
3. If you had to describe God in three words, what would they be?
4. If you had to describe your childhood in three words, what would they be?

TOWER POWER
Rich Cotton

This is an active learning exercise that takes less than thirty minutes and helps a developing group to cultivate relationship-building skills.

1. Divide into groups of three or four people who do not know each other well.

2. Distribute one magazine, one newspaper section, one pencil, one ten-inch piece of string and five paper clips to each group, giving at least one item to each person.

3. Read the following directions:

You have just entered the Tower Culture in a very wet and often flooded area of the world. Homes in this area are in the form of a tower to keep the family up and out of the floods and away from certain reptiles or animals that may seek refuge in your home. The family who uses their resources most efficiently in the form of the tallest tower is ascribed much honor, reverence and wisdom as leaders of the village.

Each group is a family in a newly founded village. Each family member has a component needed for the building of your family tower. You have the power to decide how your component should be best used in building the tower. Your goal as a family is to build the tallest tower from the floor up that will allow you special leadership and privileges as the most respected and needed family. You have eight minutes to make decisions and complete the building of your family tower. The prestige of the family with the tallest tower will be translated into our weekend's culture in the form of not having to do the dishes all weekend." (Substitute another incentive if you are not at camp.)

4. Time them for eight minutes and tell them when two, four, six and eight minutes are up.

5. Measure the towers and declare the winning family.

6. Discussion questions:

   a. Which member's participation was most helpful in the team's accomplishment of the task? Why?

   b. What behaviors seemed to hinder the team's efforts?

   c. What did you learn about yourself as you had to work with a very new group of people? (Discuss feelings of trust, whether people were active or passive in their participation, problems in communication, how they reacted to stress and so on.)

d. What did you learn about other team members as you worked on this?

e. We will be working as a team in our learning, prayer and emotional support. What principles and guidelines can we follow to help us develop as a team as a result of what we learned from this simulation? Write these down for all to see on an overhead or chalkboard.

TRUST WALK

Adapted by Tom Sirinides

Divide the group into pairs. (You can use prayer partners or people who don't know each other well.) Blindfold one person in each pair. Each unblindfolded person leads a blindfolded person around the general vicinity of your meeting place. Try to provide many different experiences—take them up some stairs, go outside and inside, help them feel different objects, walk at different paces, walk on different materials (grass, floors, dirt), but say nothing after the walk has started. You must nonverbally communicate all messages. One example of this would be that when you get to some steps, stop before the step and lift their arm slightly to indicate a rise.

After about five minutes, change places, allowing the other person to become blindfolded. After another five minutes the group regathers. Discuss what kinds of feelings you had as you were blindfolded and as you touched objects. Here are some questions you can use (if you use all of them you will need twenty to thirty minutes):

- How did it feel to lead?

- Did you sense a lack of trust?

- How did you seek to build trust?

- What was difficult about leading?

- What made it hard to lead?

- Did you develop any signals?

- How did it feel to be led?

- Did you trust the other person?

- What helped you to grow in trusting them?

- Did you try to keep track of where you were all the time while blindfolded?

- Did you peek?

- What was it like to have no control over what was happening?

- Did the other person ever let go of you or leave you? If so, what did you do?

- Who preferred leading? Who preferred being led? Why?

- What did you learn about yourself in all this?

  about how you relate to and trust God?

  about how you relate to and trust other people?

TWENTY LOVES

Give each person a piece of paper. Allow a few minutes for all group members to list twenty activities they enjoy doing. Some may find they have far more than twenty; others may have trouble listing five. Encourage them to think about what they enjoy doing most. For some that may even be daydreaming.

After they have made their lists, have each make the following notations next to each item to which it applies:

A   things you prefer to do alone

P   things you prefer to do with other people; if others are involved, put names of others with whom you most enjoy this activity

$ those which cost money to do (over $1.00)

R   items that have some element of risk involved (physical or personal)

S	activities that are sedentary (more quiet or passive)
M	those that are active
C	things that take some form of communication to do
L	items you had to learn to do—a skill you had to acquire
CH	activities you did as a child
PA	activities that at least one of your parents does or did

Look at your list and rank the activities. As you look over your results, what do you notice about yourself? What repeated aspects come out, particularly in your top five? Is there anything you hadn't realized before?

Here are more specific questions you could ask:

1. Do you most enjoy doing things by yourself, with others, or both? If with others, are there people you continually enjoy being with? Friends? Family? Members of the same sex? Members of the other sex? Do you usually prefer one-to-one time, small groups or large groups?

2. Do the things you enjoy usually cost money?

3. Are you a risk taker? What kind?

4. Are you sedentary, active or a mixture?

5. Do you do many things that require communication, or are you often with people doing things that don't require communication?

6. Are there skills you have had to work at to do things you enjoy, or do you mostly enjoy things that you can do naturally?

7. What things are you enjoying that you learned as a child and that your parents did? What interests have you added or built on since childhood?

8. Looking at your list, which of these would be hardest for you to give up? Which would you miss the most if you didn't do it?

Now take about ten minutes to discuss your findings with one other person in the group. If those in the group know each other fairly well, you could stay together. Note: There are no good or bad answers in this exercise. The purpose is simply to see ourselves and to share what we see with others.

When the group pulls back together, share with the whole group what you saw about yourself, particularly if you saw something you hadn't realized or thought about before. Have each person say at least one thing he or she particularly enjoyed learning in talking with his or her partner.

UNIQUE M&M GAME
Amy Brooke

Everyone in the group takes one M&M for each person in their group (including themselves). They then each take a turn describing something they feel is unique about themselves. (Example: "I am a twin." "I've gone rock climbing.") If someone else in the group shares that experience or characteristic, both (or more) eat one M&M. This continues until people begin to run out of candy. Interesting and memorable information comes to light during this game, and people have an easier time remembering each other at future meetings. (This activity takes less than fifteen minutes.)

WARM UP

Explain to the group that the following questions will help them get to know one another better. They are not loaded questions; they simply represent a way to get to know each other in a short time. (This activity takes less than an hour.)

Take one set of questions at a time. The leader can begin by answering first; then go around the circle with each answering each set of questions. If time is short and this is not your first meeting, omit Set 1 and the first question in Set 2.

Set 1

1. What is your name? (If you did this earlier, do it again so names can be learned quickly.)

2. Where did you live between the ages of seven and twelve years?

3. What stands out most in your mind about the school you attended at that time?

Set 2

1. How many brothers and sisters were in your family during the ages of seven to twelve years?

2. During your childhood, how did you like to get warm when you were chilled or cold? Perhaps after an afternoon of skating, skiing or sliding? Or early mornings at a cabin or out camping?

Set 3

During your childhood, where did you feel the center of human warmth was? Was it a room or a person? (For example, the TV room when your family was all together? the kitchen?) It may not have been a room at all; it may have been a person around whom you sensed safeness and warmth. (The leader may want to mention that some people do not remember a center of human warmth in the home. This may put at ease people for whom this was true.) Was there another center of warmth for them?

Set 4

(This question is asked to the group as a whole, and you do not need to go in a round for this. Let people answer as they feel comfortable; some may choose not to answer at this time.) When in your life, if ever, did God become more than a word? When did he become a living being, someone who was alive in your own thinking?

(This may not be an account of a conversion. This transition in one's thinking can happen before actual conversion or after. It may have happened in conversation with a person who loved them, or in a worship service or listening to music. This is not a time of discovering the whole counsel of God, but simply a time of personal awareness.)

As you conclude this discussion, point out in summary how our different experiences bring us to different points in our growth and in our experiences now.

Although our security and acceptance begins with physical warmth and graduates to human warmth, we are never complete until we find security in God.

WHAT'S IN A NAME?

Tom Sirinides

Group members tell their full name (including middle name or Asian name) and as much as they know about it: what it means, why they were given it and so on. (This activity takes less than fifteen minutes.)

"WHO AM I?"

Make a list of eight items that identify who you are or significant aspects and roles of your life. (Examples: student, son or daughter, friend, helper, writer, critic.) Then consider each item in your list. Try to imagine how it would be if that item were no longer true for you. (For example, if you were no longer a son or daughter—loss of both parents—what would that mean to you? How would you feel? What would you do? What would your life be like?) After reviewing each item in this way, rank the items by writing a number to the right of each item. Order them according to the importance this role has to you at this time. Which would most drastically affect your life if it were taken away from you? (On a scale of 1 to 8, 1 is most important, 8 is least.)

Finally, share your results with one person in your group. Tell each other how you came to your decisions. Be as open as you can. Then regather as a group. Discuss the following: Is there something about yourself this exercise has taught you? As you thought over the questions of loss of an item, did you realize some things you hadn't before? What role is most significant for you? Why? Then let the person you talked with tell the group one thing he or she appreciated about you from what you said. (This activity takes less than an hour.)

WHOPPER

Stephanie Moser

Group members are given a piece of paper, on which they write four things about themselves. Three must be true, and one must be a whopper that is disguised to sound true. Everyone reads their list, and each person tries to guess which statement is the whopper. (This activity takes less than fifteen minutes.)

ZOO
Tom Sirinides

Each person answers the questions, What animal are you most similar to? Why? (This activity takes less than fifteen minutes.)

IDEAS FOR SHAKE-UP

These ideas are specifically designed to help the group process conflict and deepen their trust.

BLESSING
Stephanie Moser

After the group has known each other quite a while (maybe four months or a semester), focus on one person at a time, and have everyone share adjectives or words that describe how you have seen God in their life. It is a time of affirming who they are and the qualities God has given them. After five to ten minutes on that person, offer prayers of thanksgiving for him or her.

COMMUNITY EVALUATION
Mike Mack

The evaluation on page 46 could be used at any stage of group life but will be particularly helpful as a tool for discussion during transition and conflict stages. Each member of the group should complete this evaluation individually. Prayerfully, honestly and humbly answer each question for your group. Circle the number from 1 to 5 that best describes your group for that attribute, 1 being "not at all" and 5 being "completely." Remember that the attribute applies to how the *entire* group practices it, not just the leader. (For instance, under "Instruct one another," consider how everyone contributes to instructing others.) Then gather together as a group and discuss

Each of the following are imperatives or directives for community from the New Testament. For each, ask yourself, "How is our small group doing?"

1. "Encourage one another daily" (Hebrews 3:13).

   1   2   3   4   5

2. "Spur one another on toward love and good deeds" (Hebrews 10:24).

   1   2   3   4   5

3. "Be at peace with each other" (Matthew 9:50).

   1   2   3   4   5

4. "Accept one another, then, just as Christ accepted you" (Romans 15:7).

   1   2   3   4   5

5. "Submit to one another out of reverence for Christ" (Ephesians 5:21).

   1   2   3   4   5

6. "Honor one another above yourselves" (Romans 12:10).

   1   2   3   4   5

7. "Instruct one another" (Romans 15:14).

   1   2   3   4   5

8. "Admonish one another" (Colossians 3:16).

   1   2   3   4   5

9. "Serve one another in love" (Galatians 5:13).

   1   2   3   4   5

10. "Forgive whatever grievances you may have against one another" (Colossians 3:13).

   1   2   3   4   5

11. "Confess your sins to each other" (James 5:16).

   1   2   3   4   5

12. "Pray for each other so that you may be healed" (James 5:16).

   1   2   3   4   5

13. "Love one another deeply, from the heart" (1 Peter 1:22).

   1   2   3   4   5

14. "Offer hospitality to one another without grumbling" (1 Peter 4:9).

   1   2   3   4   5

15. "Each one should use whatever gift he has received to serve others" (1 Peter 4:10).

   1   2   3   4   5

your choices for each attribute. Try to come to a consensus as to how you are doing. You might want to redo the evaluation as a group. For areas where the group scores a 3 or below, decide how you can improve in that area. Be specific!

INSIDE/OUTSIDE
Tom Sirinides

Have the following ready: a lunch bag for each person, newspapers and magazines, tape or glue, and scissors. Let people cut out words and pictures from the newspapers and magazines that have something to do with them. On the outside of the bag put things that describe the way you think others see you; on the inside put things that describe the way you see yourself.

SOCIOGRAM

Each person in your group relates to each other person in a unique way. There are some in your group who are very close; there are others who hardly know each other. It will help you in ministering to your group if you know where there is strength in relationships and where there are needs. Making a sociogram is one way to find out. Some observations will be evident; others may not be. More than likely, group members' feelings about these dynamics will not be known.

You can approach making a sociogram in two ways: (1) You can do it alone or with a coleader, small group coordinator or staffworker. In this way you can pinpoint some needs and look for ways to help build relationships. In the same light you can see how the group has helped build relationships. Doing a sociogram at least two to three times a year will help you track growth. (2) You can work through a sociogram with your group. Having the whole group involved in this process can give additional (and often more accurate) information. It also can lead to discussing interpretation on why some problems and feelings involving the findings may exist. As a group, you can then be committed to building a more solid community.

To make a sociogram:

1. Make a circle (females) and square (males) for each member in your group. Arrange them in a circle.

2. Put the initials of each person in a circle or square.

3. Draw:

• A heavy line to indicate a strong relationship.

• A dotted line to indicate a weak but growing relationship.

• An arrow to indicate a relationship which seems to be stronger one way than the other. (B seems to sense a stronger relationship than A).

• A wavy line to indicate tension, personality clash or antagonism.

• No line if there is no relationship between one person and another.

• A dotted line around the circle or square if the person seems alienated from the group in some way.

• Solid lines to show amount of interaction while in the group.

= little interaction

= much interaction, perhaps dominating

• Squares and circles outside the group which indicate close relationships that may or may not take members away from the group. (See p. 49)

4. Mark prayer partnerships ("PP").

5. Also, as you look at the group you may

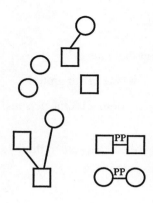

want to note the following characteristics:

- Personality distinctives (introvert-extrovert, melancholic and so on).

- Who takes the most initiative in discussions?

- Who takes initiative in unstructured times?

- Who takes the least initiative in each situation?

- Who is open about him- or herself? Who is beginning to open up?

- Identify real needs of the group.

- Identify potential growth in the group.

6. What do you do with this information?

If you make a sociogram by yourself or with one other person:

- List the obvious (people who are not closely relating to anyone in the group or tensions in the group).

- Look at your resources for dealing with these needs. Is there a relationship forming? Is there tension, and is one of these people an initiator? Who could take initiative in beginning to work through some problems? Does the group need some more fun times together? Who is your social organizer?

- Begin to talk with some of these people about the needs you see and how they could be of help in this.

- Pray for love, wisdom and guidance as you pray through each relationship and take steps to grow.

If you make a sociogram as a group, ask:

- What new things have you seen about yourself or the group as a result of this exercise?

- How did this make you feel?
- What do you see as the needs of the group?
- What resources do we have as a group to meet these needs?
- What should we do to strengthen the community life of our group?
- Is this a good time to make a covenant as a group or to set some personal goals?

Keep your notes and your sociogram and make another one in three to four months to see if your group has changed its patterns in any way.

TOUGH QUESTIONS
Shawn Isenhoff

If you are in a transition phase in which attendance is lagging or you are trying to incorporate new members, the following idea may be helpful. Have each active small group member call someone who was not at the most recent meeting and discuss the next week's study topic with that person. The active member would raise a question or issue from the upcoming study material that they found challenging or particularly interesting. At the next meeting, compile those questions and answer as many as possible at the end of the study that were not already answered through discussion of the evening. This activity encourages the active members to study God's Word prior to the meeting and lets people on the fringe know the group cares.

IDEAS FOR LIVE-IT-UP
These exercises will help you with self-disclosure, relating and celebrating one another's gifts.

COLOR ME
As your group members are getting closer you may need to encourage them to share feelings about each other more. This exercise can help.

1. Take time for each person to think of a color he or she would use to

describe each person in the group.

2. Take a piece of paper and put your name on the top. Pass the paper randomly so each person can put the color he or she associates with you on it. Then return the sheet to the person whose name is on the top.

3. Let one person at a time respond to the colors they've been given. Give the rest a chance to explain why they gave a certain color, particularly if it differs from what others have given.

4. Each can ask for clarification as needed.

If you want to be more direct, you could ask what feeling you have when you think of each individual person in your group. Then go around and give this feedback. If there are feelings that need to be worked on—hurt, distance, hostility—talk about it and confront any problems. (If your group is ready for this, it could create a much closer community and move you to the live-it-up phase.)

DINE TOGETHER
Sue Sage

As a closure celebration, you might prepare a fancy dinner for the group. Some more creative twists have been to dine in a church fellowship hall, to have someone act as chauffeur and come to pick all the members up and transport them to the dinner, and to use the time for the members to affirm each other.

DISCOVER EACH OTHERS' SPIRITUAL GIFTS

"And his gifts were . . . to equip the saints for the work of the ministry, for building up the body of Christ" (Ephesians 4:11-12 RSV). Take time to help people identify gifts God has given them and how each can be used in your fellowship. (The figure on page 52 will guide you through the process.)

Encourage each other to use gifts by providing opportunities to use them in your group or helping people get involved in the life of your chapter or church. Help those who do not realize their capabilities to do so. Group encouragement and feedback is one of the most effective ways to do this.

Read Romans 12:6-8. Then respond to the following questions.

Things I like to do for others:

1.

2.

3.

4.

5.

Things I do that God seems to bless:

1.

2.

3.

People I would like to be like:

1.

2.

3.

4.

What abilities (gifts) do these people have that I admire?

1.

2.

3.

4.

What do other people affirm about apparent gifts God has given me? (Ideally, your small group will take time to share with each member the gifts they have observed and tell what they have appreciated about their use in the small group. If it is not possible to do this in a group, an individual can try to recall what others have appreciated.)

1.

2.

3.

4.

5.

Plan to practice (for their improvement) the gifts you seem to have.

What?	When?	Where?
1.		
2.		
3.		
4.		
5.		

ENCOURAGERS
Priscilla Luming

Do a secret encouragement project for the leaders or staff by sending small gifts, Bible verses and thank yous from other members.

EVALUATE GROWTH
Dan Lentz

How do you know if you are being transformed rather than just informed? One way to evaluate our journey toward Christlikeness is to look at the characteristics of Jesus in the New Testament and ask some useful questions.

- *Are we becoming more or less judgmental than we were a year ago?* As soon as we start to pursue Christlikeness, we begin to wonder why others aren't as Christlike as we are.

- *Are we becoming more approachable, or less?* In Jesus' day, lepers, prostitutes and tax collectors were especially careful to steer clear of rabbis, who were considered especially close to God. Rabbis had the mistaken notion that their spirituality required them to distance themselves from people. Jesus was the most approachable person they had ever seen. His spirituality attracted people to him. Is it attracting people to you and your group?

- *Are we growing tired of pursuing spiritual growth, or are we energized and fulfilled by that pursuit?* The pursuit of righteousness is always exhausting when it seeks a distorted goal with distorted effort. The temptation is to throw our own effort into religious duty rather than letting the love, joy and peace of God rule in our minds.

- *Are we measuring our spiritual life only in superficial ways?* Do I tend to judge my spiritual progress more by how routinely I have prayed, completed my Bible study and attended church, or do I judge my spiritual progress by whether I love a difficult individual more than I did last year at this time?

Allow time for group members to reflect on these questions individually and then discuss what you discover about yourselves. Take this opportunity to develop personal and group goals that will allow God to work his transformation process in your lives.

GROUP JOURNAL
Paul Thigpen (adapted from The Small Group Letter, *issue 3, vol. 10)*

Encourage group members to make a journal entry in a notebook each week after they get home from the meeting or allow time for this during each meeting. Make it voluntary so that it doesn't become burdensome. You may want to decide at the beginning how long you will keep the journals.

The entries need not be long, but they should record whatever was important to the writer about what took place: what insights were gained, what decisions were made, humorous anecdotes, particular feelings about what was said or done—anything goes. Members can read their entries aloud to the group on occasion; shared observations are meaningful to a group.

HOW I RECEIVE ENCOURAGEMENT
Ann Beyerlein

On page 55 is a short exercise (*adapted from* How Do I Say I Love You?) that will help you determine what type of encouragement is most meaningful to you. Rank the types from 1 to 8, 1 being the most important to you. Then discuss this in your small group.

THE MANY SIDES OF A GROWING CHRISTIAN
Dennis R. Aquilo

Have each person fold a piece of paper into four sections, unfold it so that the whole sheet is ready to write on, and write their name at the top. Then have people fill in each of the four sections of the paper with a picture or a word that speaks to the following topics.

- Top left section: a talent they believe God has given them
- Top right section: someone they admire

- Bottom left section: a Scripture text that has great meaning and why it has meaning

- Bottom right section: something in their life that keeps them from being the Christian they want to be

Once this is done, have everyone talk about what they've written or drawn with the rest of the group.

If time allows, and the group knows one another fairly well, have them exchange papers and write one thing that they like about their brother or sister in Christ on the back of the sheet. Exchange the papers again on down the line until the sheets return to their originator.

Close by reading Romans 12:3-8 and praying with thanks to God for blessing your group and your church with the joy of one another.

QUESTION IN THE HAT
Ann Beyerlein

Each member writes down a question and puts it in a hat. The hat is passed around, and each member takes out a question and answers it.

Rank each area of encouragement
___ Meeting material needs.
___ Helping.
___ Spending time together.
___ Meeting emotional needs.
___ Saying it with words.
___ Saying it with touch.
___ Being on the same side.
___ Bringing out the best.

Complete each sentence.
When down and in need of support, I like someone to . . .
It hurts my feelings most when someone does not . . .
I feel a sense of acceptance and worth when someone . . .

How I receive encouragement. Permission is granted to photocopy this page for small group use. Taken from *Small Group Idea Book*, Cindy Bunch, ed., rev. ed. © 2003 by InterVarsity Press.

SENTENCE COMPLETION
Nina Thiel

Choose enough sentences for everyone in the group, fold them up, and put them in a hat. Send the hat around and have everyone pick one. Then have people complete their sentences.

I feel comfortable with people who . . .

I know I can trust someone when . . .

I feel cared about when . . .

I feel lonely when . . .

A friend is someone who . . .

When I am sad, it helps if someone . . .

The people I'm closest to . . .

It's hard for me to open up to people when . . .

In a group I like to . . .

At times I am afraid to reach out to others because . . .

If I could improve my relationship with others, I would . . .

SO WHAT? NOW WHAT?
Dan Lentz

One useful approach to your group time is to ask "So what?" questions regularly and systematically, but ask "Now what?" questions sparingly, yet with focus and detail when you do ask it. "So what?" invites group members to think about the implications of what they are studying. "Now what?" asks them to take action individually or together, to do something concrete about those implications. A "So what?" question might ask, "What do you conclude about God's nature by the way Jesus responded to the Samaritan woman at the well (that is, a person of another race and gender)?" A "Now what?" question might ask, "What will I do to become significantly more compassionate toward other people by this time next year?"

There is nothing more exciting than when you can look back and see this kind of life change occurring in the lives of those in your group.

VALENTINE'S DAY
Nina Thiel

Draw a heart on a half sheet of paper and divide it into five sections. (Two or three hearts can fit on one sheet.) Photocopy them on pink or red paper, cut them out and give one to each member. Complete each of the sentences below, writing your responses in the sections. After giving some time to answer the questions, each person can share his or her heart.

- Someone who really loves me is . . .

- Love is . . .

- I feel loved when . . .

- I would be more loving if I . . .

- Someone I really love is . . .

A diagram of my heart

WE MISSED YOU

Carlie Lai Fongching

Have the group send a greeting to others within the church who may be ill or absent or who have something to celebrate like a birthday or an anniversary. This is great for a large church or fellowship in which people don't all know each other. Care and love can spread from the small group to the whole community.

IDEAS FOR WRAP-UP

These ideas are designed to help the group affirm one another's gifts, experience closure and celebrate what God has done in the group.

APPRECIATION DEMONSTRATION

Sara Keiper

Each person takes enough blank sheets of paper for everyone in the group. On one side draw a picture, Bible verse, prayer, word, phrase, sentence or whatever will show the person what you have appreciated about them. On the other side of the paper draw a picture, Bible verse, prayer, words or whatever will demonstrate what you wish or hope for them.

FOOT WASHING

Sue Sage

This is a simple yet powerful way of expressing care for someone. Take a basin and towel, go around the circle and have each wash the feet of the person next to them. This goes well with a small group worship time or when studying the crucifixion.

GIFT GIVING

Sara Keiper

A week or so in advance, talk about giving gifts to show appreciation of each other and what you have experienced together. Giving a gift does not necessarily mean buying one. The best ones are usually made. A gift could be a special Bible verse made into a book mark, a certificate to do laundry for a specified period of time or a picture from a magazine that is symbolic—the possibilities are limitless. Encourage people not to buy things, or at the very least, set a cost limit. (For some, choosing to buy can be significant.)

Have one person sit in the center of your small group circle. Each person then gives to this person an intangible gift or Bible verse that reflects something they would like to see them have, an area in which they would like to see them grow, or a reminder of a special time or quality. Give the gift and explain why you are giving that gift. Each member of the group takes turns being in the center. Close in a time of thanksgiving and prayer for one another. You may want to lay hands on each person as you pray for them.

GIFT MAKING
Nina Thiel

A week before the group's last time together for the semester, have everyone draw names and spend the week making a gift, such as a bookmark, card, hand-painted T-shirt, poster or keepsake box. You might also pick out one special verse from the book of the Bible you have been studying or based on a character from Scripture and offer a blessing: "May you be like ____, who . . ." For example, see Ruth 4:11-12.

GROUP HISTORY
Paul Thigpen (Adapted from The Small Group Letter, *vol. 10, issue 3.)*

A great idea for groups that have been together for a long time or are ending, this project offers a sense of closure and puts things into perspective. Either at home or in a meeting each member writes a summary of his or her experience in the group as if it were a chapter in a history book. Focus on fond memories, critical junctures and the overall patterns of the group's experience. What was the happiest moment in the group? What challenges were overcome? What directions or central concerns took shape as the group developed? What are the most important lessons learned? What contribution has the group made to their relationship with God? Allow people to keep their writing private if they want to.

GROWTH

Have each member discuss one area where they have been growing during the past three or so months together. Then have them look ahead into the next three months. Ask, "In what one area would you like to see yourself grow most (or continue growing most)?" Pray as a group for each person's continued growth.

MEMORIAL STONES
Sara Keiper

This comes from Joshua 4. Bring enough rocks (not gigantic ones) for everyone in the group. Have each person pick one. Read Joshua 4, or tell the story and read just a few verses in summary. Then have each person tell ways they have seen God's faithfulness, and place their rock on the growing pile. Conclude your time thanking God for his faithfulness.

Variation: Bring markers and have people write a word or draw something symbolizing God's faithfulness. After making the memorial and praying, let people take their rocks home as a visual reminder of God's faithfulness.

PEOPLE CELEBRATIONS
Sue Sage

Spend time as a small group celebrating a certain person's life. Celebrations usually include the whole group eating that person's favorite meal while listening to the music of their choice and coaxing out of them some childhood stories. Sometimes this is followed by doing that person's favorite activity. Some celebrations have included handmade gifts for that person and usually include a time of prayer for them.

PRAY SCRIPTURE
Sara Keiper

Using prayers and other Scriptures, pray specifically for each person in your group. Prepare for this by asking God to lead you to particular passages for each person. Another way to do this is to let the group pick out prayers for each other, or let each person choose what they want the group to pray for them.

Here are just a few suggested passages: Numbers 6:24-34; Deuteronomy 33:26-29; Psalms 20 and 67; Isaiah 43:1-5; Lamentations 3:22-23; Romans 8:38-39; Ephesians 1:17-19; 3:14-19; 5:15-20; Philippians 1:6; 1:9-11; 3:12-14; 4:4-6, 8-10; Colossians 1:9-12; 1 Timothy 6:11-12; 1 Peter 5:6-7. You may also want to choose a passage from the book you've been studying in the group.

STRENGTH BOMBARDMENT

This exercise is designed to let you express the positive feelings you have for each other by pointing out the strengths you see in others. This is best done after you have gotten to know each other fairly well.

First, ask one person to remain silent while the others concentrate on this person and bombard him or her with all of the things that you like or see as a strength. Keep bombarding the first person with positive feelings until you run out of words. Then, move on to the next person in your group and do the same until you have covered everyone in your group.

After everyone has finished, ask, "How did you feel when you were the focus of bombardment? Don't evaluate what was said about you, but tell how you felt about getting the feedback." Then ask, "How did you feel about giving feedback to others?"

THANK-YOU NOTES
Sara Keiper

Give each person attractive pieces of stationery so that each one has enough sheets for a note to all of the others in the group. Have people write words of appreciation, a Bible verse or whatever else they are thankful for. Have each person be "it." Each one in the group reads their note to that person, followed by a group prayer thanking God for him or her.

A TICKET FOR YOUR THOUGHTS
Nina Thiel

Everyone in the small group gets a ticket, and no one can be asked a question twice until everyone has been asked a question once. Questions can range from light to deep, and the answerer has the right to ask for a different question if they feel uncomfortable with the one they are first asked.

 This TICKET entitles the bearer to the answer to one question of his/her choice when given to another member of his/her small group Bible study.

Ticket for your thoughts

YEARBOOK PAGE
Nina Thiel

Ask someone to take a picture of the whole small group well before your last time together for the semester or year. Develop and make enough copies for everyone. Glue the photographs on nice pieces of cardstock. Include the names of everyone in your small group, the year, and so on. At your last time together, bring out the cards plus lots of pens and give everyone a chance to write on each other's pages.

BOOKS AND BIBLE STUDIES ON COMMUNITY

Arnold, Jeffrey. *The Big Book on Small Groups.* Rev. ed. Downers Grove, Ill.: InterVarsity Press, 2003. A wonderful overview of how to lead small groups, with an emphasis on community. The appendix at the back includes Bible studies for your first four small group meetings.

Bonhoeffer, Dietrich. *Life Together.* Translated by John Doberstein. New York: Harper & Row, 1984. Classic account of the experience of Christian community in an underground seminary during the Nazi years. Discusses the role of prayer, worship, work and service in community.

Crabb, Larry. *Connecting: Healing for Ourselves and Our Relationships.* Nashville: Word, 1997. A vision for the healing capacity of Christian relationships.

Griffin, Em. *Getting Together.* Downers Grove, Ill.: InterVarsity Press, 1982. A guide for groups of all sorts to discover what makes a group good. Covers conflict, deviance, persuasion, expectations, leadership and how to have a good discussion.

Icenogle, Gareth. *Biblical Foundations for Small Group Ministry.* Downers Grove, Ill.: InterVarsity Press, 1994. An in-depth biblical survey of Christian community and how it works in small groups.

Lofink, Gerhard. *Jesus & Community.* Philadelphia: Fortress, 1984. Jesus' model of forming community with the disciples.

Peck, M. Scott. *A Different Drum: Community Making & Peace.* New York: Touchstone, 1988. The author describes his journey toward finding community with several different groups.

Snyder, Howard. *The Community of the King.* Rev. ed. Downers Grove, Ill.: InterVarsity Press, 2004. Explores the relationship between the kingdom of God and the church in our daily lives.

Sterk, Andrea, and Peter Scazzero. *Christian Community.* LifeGuide® Bible Study. Downers Grove, Ill.: InterVarsity Press, 1994. Twelve studies on what Christ's body, the church, is designed to be and how we find our gifts and experience worship, healing and God's power.

Swihart, Judson J. *How Do You Say, "I Love You"?* Downers Grove, Ill.: InterVarsity Press, 1977. Describes eight different languages of love. Especially for married couples, but others can benefit.

PART TWO

WORSHIP AND PRAYER

Experiences of worship and prayer can be powerful in a small group. Most groups include prayer at the end of each meeting. There are ideas here to encourage members to pray and to make that time significant. However, your small group can also go much deeper into experiences of worship and celebration together. You can make these activities a part of your regular meeting—times of silence and worship can be a great way to help people get settled and focused at the beginning of a meeting. You might also want to consider devoting a whole session just to worship from time to time or even taking a retreat to-gether to grow in worship. The ideas are organized alphabetically.

ATTRIBUTES OF GOD

Carol Johnson

Go around the group having each person take the next letter in the alphabet to describe an attribute of God. Read Psalm 145.

BIBLE REFLECTION

Look back at the passage you have studied and ask what things it has shown you about God or what attributes you see of God in this passage. Praise him for these aspects of his character and person.

The Book of Common Prayer

This historical resource of the church is full of material that can be used to guide a group into worship and prayer. Following are a few excerpts you can use.

A General Thanksgiving

Accept, O Lord, our thanks and praise for all that you have done for us. We thank you for the splendor of the whole creation, for the beauty of this world, for the wonder of life, and for the mystery of love.

We thank you for the blessing of family and friends, and for the loving care which surrounds us on every side.

We thank you for setting us at tasks which demand our best efforts, and for leading us to accomplishments which satisfy and delight us.

We thank you also for those disappointments and failures that lead us to acknowledge our dependence on you alone.

Above all, we thank you for your Son Jesus Christ; for the truth of his Word and the example of his life; for his steadfast obedience, by which he overcame temptation; for his dying, through which he overcame death; and for his rising to life again, in which we are raised to the life of your kingdom.

Grant us the gift of your spirit, that we may know him and make him known; and through him, at all times and in all places, may give thanks to you in all things. *Amen.*

Corporate Confession (*contemporary form*)

Most merciful God,

we confess that we have sinned against you

in thought, word, and deed,

by what we have done,

and by what we have left undone.

We have not loved you with our whole heart;

we have not loved our neighbors as ourselves.

We are truly sorry and we humbly repent.

For the sake of your Son Jesus Christ,

have mercy on us and forgive us;

that we may delight in your will,

and walk in your ways,

to the glory of your Name. Amen.

BREAK WITH TRADITION

Doing things differently can enhance your time of worship. Perhaps plan to meet at a neighborhood church one evening and use the sanctuary or chapel as a place of worship. Kneel as you pray. Lift your hands to God. Take a nature walk and pray as you walk together, thanking God for what you see in his creation. Use creative dance or drama as a form of worship. Be original.

CONCERTS OF PRAYER

John Rogers, Marie Paretti and Jeff Yourison (Adapted from International Fellowship of Evangelical Students and Student Leadership, *Winter 1993.)*

Your group can commit to spending several hours on a Saturday morning or a weekend evening or even a whole day or night in prayer for the world. InterVarsity students may want to commit to spending time in prayer for the work of IFES (the International Fellowship of Evangelical Students) around the world. Church members may want to pray for the missions program of their denomination. Or group members may want to pray for friends who are missionaries. Prayers might also focus on national and international revival. Here are a few steps to putting it together.

Step 1. Mark the Date

World Student Day is February 24. The National Day of Prayer is the first Thursday in May. Various denominations have designated days of prayer for their ministries.

Step 2. Choose the Planners

Your group may want to plan the event for a larger group of people or for yourselves. Be sure to plan prayerfully and with good communication. Get input from the prayer warriors in your group and any ministry teams that might play a role.

Step 3. Use Existing Structures

Make the concert of prayer part of a regular meeting or time of worship.

Step 4. Get Information on the Group You Are Praying For

Invite missionaries or Christian international students to come and speak. Check out resources from your denomination. *Operation World* by Patrick Johnstone has significant facts about missionary movements in every part of the world as well as information on planning concerts of prayer. Consider how to provide this information during the course of your time of prayer to help participants know how to pray.

Step 5. Plan Creatively

Use ideas that fit your context. Here are a few that have worked in the past:

- Reserve a comfortable place on campus or in your church to pray throughout the day, and have people sign up for shifts during the day so that a continual prayer goes up to God.

- Organize an extended meeting time for a large or small group including times of worship and praise, singing, silent and vocal prayer. Break into smaller groups at times then return to the larger group.

- Invite churches in your area to join in or have their own concerts of prayer on the same day.

- Develop a short talk or skit to describe the ministry you are praying for and how your group fits into the bigger picture.

- Bring in needs and concerns you notice in newspapers and magazines. Pray for specific local needs as well as global needs.

- Find out what a day in the life of a person from a country you are praying for would be like. You might have a meal together to sample the food from a particular country.

- Have a world map on hand, and mark it to show unreached countries and specific places you're praying for.

- Take an offering to support a missionary in another country.

Step 6. Plan Effective Follow-Up

Encourage people to keep praying, perhaps by organizing a monthly or weekly prayer meeting. Get involved in a partnering relationship with a church or IFES chapter in another country. See the section on revival prayer. You may want to commit to this discipline individually or as a group.

CREATE A PSALM
Kelle Ashton

Begin by reading a few psalms that are meaningful to you. Then have everyone in the group write the first verse of any psalm on the top of a piece of paper. Each person passes their paper to the right. The next person reads the verse and adds one to it from their own thoughts, trying to build on the previous verse. Continue passing the papers around until everyone has added to each psalm. Read each psalm in the group.

Jane Bacon of California suggests another psalm writing method based on Psalm 107: After reading Psalm 107, look at the four categories of people described there (vv. 4-9, 10-16, 17-22, 23-32). Note the format in each of these groups of verses:

Some _____ (description of people).
They were _____ (description of sinful actions).
Then they cried out to the Lord and he delivered them from_____

_____.

Let them give thanks for _____ (God's work).
Challenge each person to write their own stanza of this psalm or several stanzas describing periods of their life. Then, read it to the group. End in praise for how God continues to know us, hear our cries and deliver us.

DEVOTIONAL READINGS

J. I. Packer's *Knowing God*, A. W. Tozer's *The Knowledge of the Holy* and J. B. Phillips's *Your God Is Too Small* are excellent choices for devotional readings. Read short excerpts that will direct your thoughts to God, and give time for the group to respond in worship. Use books of prayer such as *The Book of Common Prayer*. These prayers can open or close times of prayer. Richard Foster has put together spiritual readings that show how great men and women of the faith have responded to the character of God.

Here's an excerpt from *Knowing God* (pp. 41-42):

What matters supremely is not the fact that I know God, but the larger fact which underlies it—the fact that *he knows me*. I am graven on the palms of his hands. I am never out of his mind. All my knowledge of him depends on his sustained initiative in knowing me. I know him because he first knew me, and continues to know me. he knows me as a friend, one who loves me; and there is no moment when his eye is off me, or his attention distracted from me, and no moment, therefore, when his care falters.

This is momentous knowledge. There is unspeakable comfort— the sort of comfort that energizes, be it said, not enervates—in knowing that God is constantly taking knowledge of me in love, and watching over me for my good. There is tremendous relief in knowing that his love to me is utterly realistic, based at every point on prior knowledge of the worst about me, so that no discovery now can disillusion him about me, in the way I am so often disillusioned about myself, and quench his determination to bless me.

There is, certainly, great cause for humility in the thought that he sees all the twisted things about me that my fellow-men do not see (and am I glad!), and that he sees more corruption in me than that which I see in myself (which, in all conscience, is enough). There is, however, equally great incentive to worship and love God in the thought that, for some unfathomable reason, he wants me as his friend, and desires to be my friend, and has given his Son to die for me in order to realize this purpose. We cannot work these thoughts out here, but merely to mention them is enough to show how much it means to know not merely that we know God, but that he knows us.

EXAMINE YOUR CONSCIENCE
St. Ignatius of Loyola

In *The Spiritual Exercises of St. Ignatius* we find a five-point method for "the daily examination of conscience" in prayer. This can be used in your group, and you can challenge one another to keep this discipline personally.

1. I thank you_____ .

2. I need you _____ .

3. I love you_____ .

4. I am sorry_____ .

5. Stay with me, Lord!

FASTING
Northwestern University students

The Bible defines fasting as a Christian's voluntary abstinence from food for spiritual purposes. Jesus makes it clear that he expects us to fast. In Matthew 6:16 he begins by saying, "When you fast." Also, this teaching about fasting in the Sermon on the Mount directly follows his teaching on giving and praying. It is as if it were assumed that giving, praying and fasting are all part of the Christian devotion.

We cannot use fasting to impress God (or others) or to earn his acceptance. We are made acceptable to God through Jesus' work, not ours. Fasting pointedly reveals the things that control us, whether that be our stomachs, pride, anger, bitterness, jealousy, selfishness, fear—the list goes on. Fasting reminds us that, instead, we are sustained "by every word that proceeds from the mouth of God" (Matthew 4:4). Food does not sustain us; God sustains us. When the disciples, assuming that he was hungry, brought lunch to Jesus, he said, "I have food to eat that you know nothing about. . . . My food . . . is to do the will of him who sent me and to finish his work" (John 4:32, 34).

Richard Foster writes in *Celebration of Discipline*:

> Therefore, in experiences of fasting we are not so much abstaining from food as we are feasting on the word of God. Fasting is feasting! . . . We are told not to act miserable when fasting because, in point of fact, we are not miserable. We are feeding on God, and just like the Israelites who were sustained in the wilderness by the miraculous manna from heaven, so we are sustained by the word of God.

Fasting does not change God's hearing so much as it changes our praying. There's something about it that sharpens and gives passion to our intercessions. Fasting also makes us more receptive to God's guidance and wisdom. The church in Antioch "fasted and prayed" before they laid their hands on Barnabas and Saul and sent them off on the first missionary journey (Acts 13:3).

There are also many other purposes of fasting such as expressing grief, seeking deliverance or protection, expressing repentance and a return to God, humbling oneself before God, overcoming temptation, expressing love and worship to God, and so on. In all of this, God will reward those who diligently pursue him.

A small group could decide to do a prayer fast together beginning after lunch on a given day. During the dinner hour, the following Bible study could be used.

1. Read through Psalm 145 and jot down all the characteristics of God you see in the passage.

2. Take some time to praise God for the characteristics in the passage.

3. Then read Acts 4. Below are some prayer requests based on that passage.

- *Personal:* that knowledge of Scripture would grow for God's glory (vv. 8-11), that we would have the boldness and courage of Peter and John to speak to friends and neighbors about Christ (vv. 19-20)

- *Christian community:* that prayer would be the first thing on our minds (v. 24), that the Holy Spirit would shake us to speak the word of God boldly (v. 31), that we would exemplify the community of believers to our community (vv. 32-35)

- *Community:* that people in our neighborhoods and on our campuses would recognize their sinfulness (v. 10), that people would acknowledge that Jesus is salvation (v. 12), that Jesus would reside in our community (vv. 29-30)

That evening a small group could meet to process the day, discuss what God has taught them and pray together again.

FILL IN THE BLANK

Small Group Network

Use fill-in-the-blank prayers to help people get more comfortable with praying aloud. Have participants fill in words to short phrases such as "God is _____." Then have each person say his or her completed phrase. Next have them fill in the blank with the same word for this phrase: "God, you are _____." Again, have each person say his or her phrase. Then say, "Congratulations, you just prayed!" You can do a similar exercise using psalms but having participants put their own word(s) in particular places. For instance, use Psalm 8:1: "I love you, O Lord, my _____." Or Psalm 23: "The Lord is my _____, I shall not _____."

GOD HUNT

Karen Mains

Spend a few minutes reflecting on the past week looking for times that God has worked in your life, answered a prayer or been present in a way you overlooked at the time. Listen to each person's experience, then pray in praise for these things. For more ideas on how to discern God at work in our lives see *The God Hunt* by Karen Mains.

GUIDED REFLECTION

adapted from Doug Stewart by Northwestern University students

Something like this could be used on a small group retreat or in a session devoted to worship and meditation. After the group comes back together after a time of personal reflection:

1. Read and ponder Psalm 107 as an example of remembering, reflecting and learning from God's interventions in our history.

2. Draw in a lifeline of the flows and movements of your spiritual life over the past three or six months. Fill in significant events and activities. Express the "high" as well as the "low" periods.

- What characterized the "high" periods? What characterized the "low" periods? Remember what was happening in and around you at those times. Do you see any constants or patterns?

- What have been recurring or major struggles in your life this past year? Any painful failures?

- What growth or progress have you seen take place in your life?

3. Remember that growth in grace often seems to be like going backwards as we discover new areas of need and experience new grace. This is often as we go through hard, often embarrassing and painful experiences. In the midst of this, we find grace to cover us and to carry us through. Often too, the awareness of growth is known only to us and is not so visible to others. Growth can take the form of seeing recurring areas of defeat lessen their hold on us. Growth can be seen as old fears are faced and set aside, or as old wounds are acknowledged and healing begins. Old patterns (often from childhood) are acknowledged and renounced, and new patterns are initiated. Some constants of true growth in grace are

- deepening trust in God as we face life's threats, choices and uncertainties.

- deepening awareness and experience of the love of God toward us, resulting in more freedom and inner wholeness.

- deepening, more resilient hope in God's promises and power in the face of the forces of evil that confront us and that result in more patience and steadfastness.

    4. Try to summarize a couple of the basic things that God has been showing you or teaching you during this time. What significant decisions or turning points have you come to?

    5. Write down specific blessings received, for which you can give thanks and praise to God. Be ready to share one of these blessings with the small group this day.

HEALING PRAYER

Roy Lawrence (taken from The Practice of Christian Healing)

The laying on of hands has always had a central place in the ministry of Christian healing. It is natural to touch those who we are seeking to help or comfort. When a little boy falls and scuffs this knee and comes weeping into the kitchen to his mother, she knows naturally that it is not sufficient to stand at the other end of the room and tell him he will be all right. She instinctively sits him on her knee, gives his leg a rub and says "It will be better, now," and so it is! There is healing in a loving touch.

Scripture tells us that Jesus incorporated this natural ingredient of human care into the heart of his healing ministry. For instance, after the healing of Peter's mother-in-law, "When the sun was setting, the people brought to Jesus all who had various kinds of sickness, and laying his hands on each one, he healed them" (Luke 4:40). Jesus expected his followers to incorporate the laying on of hands into the heart of their healing ministry (Mark 16:18).

When I pray for someone, I put one or both hands on that person's head and pray something like "Father, let these hands of mine convey the touch of Jesus, the love of Jesus, the healing power of Jesus—(*name*) I claim all that God has in his generous heart for you here and now. God our Father and Creator recreate you by his mighty power in body, mind and spirit. God the Son, our Lord Jesus Christ, meet you at your point of need and hold you in his strong and loving presence. And the healing influence of God the Holy Spirit, Lord and Giver of Life move within you, freeing you from all that could hurt you and bringing you new life at every level of your being. The blessing of God Almighty, Father, Son and Holy Spirit rest on you, surge within you and bring you wholeness, joy and peace. Amen."

My expectation is that when there has been prayer with the laying on of hands, there will always be blessing and strengthening unless the Lord is resisted. Often the blessing and strengthening will be accompanied by some sort of physical, mental or spiritual healing. This may be either total or partial.

HYMNS AND SONGS

Instruct or remind people to think of themselves as speaking to God as they sing. Read a song rather than sing it for a change of pace. Use familiar songs at your first few meetings. Keep a list of those your group knows. Give background material if it is helpful. Have members concentrate on one or two main themes that run through the hymn. Point these out ahead of time so the group's attention is drawn into focus. Study the hymn to see what Scripture is referred to. For example, at Advent "O Come, O Come, Emmanuel" would be appropriate. At Easter "When I Survey the Wondrous Cross" or "O Sacred Head Now Wounded" would be especially meaningful. Hymns like "And Can It Be," "Jesu, Lover of My Soul," "Amazing Grace" and "O for a Thousand Tongues to Sing" call us to worship and wonder at what God has done for us. And "Guide Me, O Thou Great Jehovah" and "Be Thou My Vision" call us to commitment as we seek God's will.

INTERCESSORY PRAYER
Paul Hughes

A significant aspect of your small group will be praying for one another's needs. An intercessor is one who stands in the gap between God and the world and bears the burden to pray. Studying the following outline and passages will give you courage to exercise spiritual authority through prevailing prayer.

Entering God's Throne Room

- Enter confidently in Jesus' name (1 Timothy 2:5; Hebrews 4:14-16; 5:7-10)

- Enter continually (Luke 11:9-13; Philippians 4:6; Colossians 4:2; 2 Thessalonians 1:11)

- Enter privately (Matthew 6:5-6)

- Enter with a pure heart with no unforgiveness (Matthew 6:14-15; 2 Corinthians 2:10-11), no selfish motives (Philippians 2:3-4; James 4:3) and no unconfessed sin (James 5:16)

- Enter with others (Matthew 18:19; Acts 2:42)

- Enter with the Word of God (Daniel 9:1-3; Ephesians 6:17-18)

How to Intercede

- Pray to the Father in Jesus' name (John 14:8-14; Acts 4:5-12)

- Pray with the help of the Holy Spirit (Romans 8:26-27; Ephesians 6:17)

- Pray on the offensive with God's agenda in mind (Matthew 16:18; Ephesians 6:18)

- Know the enemy's power (Romans 8:37-39) and weapons (John 8:44; Revelation 12:10), and pray against the powers and principalities (Ephesians 6:12-13)

- Know the Lord (Luke 10:18)

- Have confidence in the blood of the Lamb (Revelation 12:11)

- Pray with worship and praise (2 Chronicles 20:18-22)

- Pray in unity with other believers (John 17:20-23)

- Combine prayer with fasting (Acts 13:2; 14:23)

JOURNALING

Completing a journaling exercise as a group and discussing it can be very rewarding. It can be an important step in introducing members to a new discipline that can be used personally as well. Here are some possible journaling topics.

- How have you been aware of God's presence in your life today? this week? this month? this year? throughout your life?

- What have you learned about God recently?

- What are your future goals—one year, five years, ten years?

- What would you say if you could ask God any question? Why?

- Describe the most significant person in your family. Is your relationship with that person positive or negative? How has it affected you?

Richard Peace has created a journaling guide especially for group use called *Spiritual Journaling*. It includes group discussion questions, journaling exercises and group Bible studies. It's a great tool for introducing a group to this spiritual discipline.

KEEP A PRAYER DIARY
Small Group Network

Maintain a prayer diary for the group. Include the date of each request, the person making the request, the need, and the date and circumstances by which the request was answered. It's fun and encouraging to look back over requests and see how they were answered.

KEEP IT SHORT
Small Group Network

To help people get comfortable, model prayer in short phrases. Ask others who usually pray out loud to also pray in short phrases. Then ask those who do not usually pray to simply say short phrases to the Lord. You may need to jump in with a short prayer, especially after someone in the group says a long-winded prayer.

LEAD WORSHIP

Dan Smith and Steven Reames

Worship can augment a small group experience, and a small group can learn from one another about what it is to worship God.

1. Be Prepared

Always, always play or sing through the songs before the group meeting in the order you plan to sing them during the actual group time. This helps you discover which songs are too high or low to sing in that particular key. It also helps you include or exclude songs if you have no instrumentation. ("Celebrate Jesus, Celebrate," for example, has long pauses between lines intended for musical fills. A lack of music and singing during this time can produce awkwardness, rightly or wrongly so.)

Other questions to consider: Do you have the proper accompaniment (guitar, piano, CD, cassette, a capella)? Do you know the songs? Do you have song sheets for those who don't know the words? If you are the musician, do you need the music in front of you? Can you lead in the correct key without a musician?

2. Be Confident

Never apologize for leading. Speak and sing distinctly. If you make a mistake, make it loud and keep on moving. Always remember that everyone expects the worship leader to lead. If you lead, they will follow. Allowing times of silence without direction can cause people to second guess what is happening; sometimes strong-willed people will interpret this as a lack of leadership and inappropriately try to move things along if they think you are faltering.

3. Be Sensitive

Leading worship requires three sets of ears: physical ears to hear how the music is progressing, mental ears to gauge the atmosphere of the group and spiritual ears to hear what the Holy Spirit is saying. Be especially sensitive for signals to move or to wait. Never rush worship or let it drag. When choosing songs, listen to the Holy Spirit; don't choose songs just because they're your favorites.

4. Be Authentic

Fix your eyes on Jesus, the author and perfecter of our faith (Hebrews 12:2). Don't let the action of leading worship become a distraction from your own worship. People will sense your authenticity or lack thereof. Focus on the Lord as much as possible. This works best when you are prepared.

5. Be Passionate

Worship demands wholehearted participation. Become wholly engaged in the worship process as you lead. Choose to do it, think about it, feel it and express it physically. Give those you are leading permission to do the same. Go with your instincts. Let people know that you care about what is happening. Always provide room for teaching people how to worship. Encourage and teach the physical expressions of worship and what they mean, both from Scripture and example.

6. Use Scripture

The book of Psalms is an excellent resource for worship. Start by having somebody read a psalm while the musician plays the first song in the background. Or, at a predesignated time (you'll have to work out a signal or a specific song), have somebody read a Scripture to meditate on between songs. If you are playing an instrument yourself, you can do this if you can play and speak simultaneously.

7. Be Positive

Focus on the character of God (holiness, love, power, etc.). This is not the time to browbeat people into a more authentic faith. Let the Holy Spirit do his own convicting. Choose songs that bring people into close relationship with God. Avoid songs with obscure, distracting, or confusing tunes or lyrics.

8. Be Brief

The average attention span of an American is thirteen minutes. Keep worship short in small groups (ten minutes or about four songs). Don't feel obligated to talk between each song. Remember that when you are talking they are not worshiping. A worship leader is an usher in the throne room of God. Your job is to bring people into his presence and then get out of the way.

9. Practice Continuity

Worship should flow as seamlessly as possible with everything else that is happening. Try to not pause between songs, but move right into the next one if possible. If it is necessary to provide a list to everybody before you start, go ahead and do that so you don't have to stop and shout out song numbers.

It is almost always best to ease out of worship rather than just abruptly ending it. If you are using an instrument, you should rarely just stop playing cold. Some ideas for segueing worship to the next portion of the meeting:

- Direct the group to take time to listen to what God is saying. You may use background instrumentation for this.

- Ask if anyone has had God already reveal something to them.

- Encourage any other gifts of the Holy Spirit.

- Have people pray words of exaltation and worship.

THE LORD'S PRAYER
Patty Pell

Use each line of the Lord's Prayer as a guide for a few minutes of group prayer. For example, after "hallowed be thy name" is read, worship by using various names for God in praise. Work through the entire prayer in this way.

MAKE IT PERSONAL
Small Group Network

Personalize a psalm or one of the great prayers from the book of Acts or one of Paul's letters. Ephesians 3:14-21 is a good one to try. Get with partners and have each person pray for the other, inserting their name into the Bible text.

MEDITATION
Stephen D. and Jacalyn Eyre

Use the "approach" exercises in Spiritual Encounter Guides by Stephen D. and Jacalyn Eyre (IVP) to help the group focus their thoughts and quietly prepare for study. Discuss your experiences before you begin the rest of the group time. Here are a few samples from *Entering God's Presence.*

- Make a list of things that are on your mind that come between you and God right now. Lift each one up to the Lord and ask him to take them.

- Joyce Huggett writes of being in God's presence and hearing God call her name. "Sometimes it seemed as though Jesus himself stood in front of me or beside me or above me. . . . The only way I can describe it is to liken it to [what] a person feels when they love someone very deeply. . . . No words are necessary. They might even be intrusive, for they could trivialize the love."

Sit quietly for a few moments. If you can enter into the silence described above, write down a few words to describe it. If you can't enter silence yet, write down the distractions that you feel and give them to the Lord.

- Imagine that you are in a desert and in need of water. You see a well in the distance and head for it. How do you feel? Now see your heart as the desert and the Lord as the well. Write down your responses.

You can also use meditation to close your group or end a Bible study. Stephen Eyre titles these sections "Reflect." Here are some samples from *Waiting on the Lord.*

- In Psalm 30 David expresses some of the ups and downs of his life. Consider the last six months to a year of your life and then chart your ups and downs.

Highs

1   2   3   4   5   6

Lows

Meditate through the ups and downs, picturing the Lord with you through each phase. Once you have done that, write down your insights and emotions.

- David writes that he has "become like broken pottery" (Psalm 31:12). At one time or another we have all felt shattered and broken by the events of life. Perhaps you still feel that way (although the events happened a long time ago). Imagine that you are a broken pot. Sit quietly for a while and allow God to put your life back together. After a time of reflection, write down your observations.

MOOD-BREAKING PRAYER
Ellen Secrest

Have you ever arrived at small group to discover a gang of grouches awaiting you? In *Daily Guideposts 1994* Ellen Secrest suggests "mood-breaker prayers" for those times. The key to these prayers is to focus on lifting up the needs of others. Soon you'll find that your mind is more in tune with God's.

NAMES OF GOD
Lisa Overby

Bring five-by-seven index cards or paper and pencils or pens for everyone, and pass them out. Ask everyone to write down all the names of God they can think of. (This can also be done with the attributes of God.) Give a time limit of three to five minutes. When everyone is done, ask those who are comfortable to list the names they have written down. As you go around, everyone can add each others' name to their lists. Each member will have a "names of God" postcard when they're done. It'll look something like this:

All-Mighty, Forgiving, Creator, Provider, Most High God, Friend, Eternal, Conqueror, Faithful, Seeker of My Heart, Always There, Peacemaker, A Prayer Away

Talk about why these names are significant to members of the group. Make this a basis for your prayer and praise.

This is very encouraging for the seeker, believer and especially the small group leader. Save the cards and do the activity again later in the year to discover how you are learning about God.

The table on page 84 lists some names of God from *Knowing God by His Names: A 31-Day Experiment* by Dick Purnell (Here's Life Publishers) to give you a sample of the riches that can be found in Scripture. Another way to use these names in worship is to encourage the group to quietly reflect on one verse or one name of God.

Passing the Peace

Names	Characteristics	Key Passage
Adam, the Last	Different from Adam and his descendants	1 Corinthians 15:45-47
Advocate	Helper, divine lawyer who pleads our case	1 John 2:1-2
Almighty	All-powerful	Revelation 1:8
Alpha and Omega	Beginning and end of everything good	Revelation 22:13
Amen	God's final seal of his promises	Revelation 3:14
Ancient of Days	Judge of the whole world	Daniel 7:9
Angel of Jehovah	Old Testament appearance of Christ	Genesis 16:7-11
Anointed	Messiah	Psalm 2:2
Apostle	The divine representative	Hebrews 3:1
Author and Perfecter of Faith	Origin of salvation, leader, developer	Hebrews 12:2

At the end of a meeting you may want to gather in a circle, join hands and pass the words of the benediction around the group—"May the peace of Christ go with you, Jim." The recipient will respond, "And also with you, Mary." This may best be used at the end of a retreat or perhaps a study where there has been significant personal discussion.

PERSONAL PET PEEVES
Irma Hider

The leader bakes green sugar cookies and makes green paper circles. Have each person write down their pet peeve about themselves—short-tempered, talks too much, envious. These are *character* issues. Then tell each other what you have written. Exchange papers with your prayer partner or someone else in the group. The other person will commit to praying for the person's pet peeve. Pray as a group that God would help you and then eat the green cookies. A few weeks later have people share how it is going *if* they want to. Do this to edify, *not* to put down those who have been struggling.

PICK A PRAYER
Small Group Network

Have group members write their prayer needs on index cards. Then put the cards into a bowl and have everyone pick a card (not their own). Have each person then pray for that need (either aloud or silently). Don't try this with a new group or one in which people feel intimidated about praying aloud.

PLAY MUSIC
Cindy Bunch

Select favorite songs of praise from contemporary Christian artists. You can learn songs together this way or simply play them to set the tone for the beginning of a meeting. You might also play classical pieces by Bach or Handel for silent reflection or find recordings of favorite hymns.

PRAY A PSALM
Allen Lincoln

One person reads a verse, then silence is allowed where people can respond vocally or quietly. People might pray a rephrase of the verse or a reminder of something else to pray for—it can be very stream-of-consciousness. After enough time has passed, the next person prays the next verse. This can be an opening to a small group meeting or be the whole meeting itself.

PRAY IN ONE VOICE
Small Group Network

In just about every country outside the United States—and in some American churches—Christians often pray their own prayers aloud all at the same time. The idea is simply to lift our individual prayers to God without worrying about others listening or trying to listen to others' prayers. Try it with the group. All participants pray low, almost under their breaths. Tell them, "No one will hear your specific words, just a murmur." The sound this makes is beautifully soothing. This form of prayer helps people keep their focus on God and keep their minds from wandering.

PRAY THE NIGHT AWAY

Keith D. Wright

If you're looking for a great way to spend an evening with your small group, try a half-night of prayer. This works best on a weekend evening, when it's most convenient for people to gather from six p.m. till midnight. The extended time allows your group to get into a deep spirit of prayer. Plan a variety of activities to keep the evening interesting. Here are some ideas to stimulate your creativity.

- *Praise.* To set the right tone for the evening—one of gratitude and expectation—begin by giving praise and thanks to God.

- *Scripture prayers.* Say prayers aloud that incorporate favorite Bible passages. Or select several prayers contained in Scripture. Read them together, or have everyone reflect silently as one person else reads aloud.

- *Sanctuary prayer blitz.* Go into the church sanctuary. Move throughout the room, asking the Lord to bless people through what happens there. For example, stand in the pulpit and pray for your preacher and his sermons. Among the pews, pray for church members. Stand at the door and pray for greeters and visitors.

- *Silent confession.* Allow people to go off alone to confess their sins to God. (You may want to provide some brief teaching on confession and guidelines for how to do this.) When you reconvene, be sure to communicate unconditional forgiveness through Christ.

- *Drive-by prayer.* Pile into cars and drive around town. Pray for schools, nursing homes, Christian ministries and churches you pass. (It's okay for the drivers to keep their eyes open!)

- *Jericho march around City Hall.* Pray for government officials and pending legislation, and that Jesus' will would be done in your city.

- *God's view.* Go to the top of your town's tallest building and pray over your city. Pray for what you see in each direction.

Wrap up with a time of reflection about your experience together. Allow twenty to thirty minutes for people to share what they learned and how they experienced God. Order pizza or sip hot chocolate at midnight to celebrate a meaningful evening in prayer.

PRAYER CHAINS
Cindy Bunch

When someone in your group has an urgent need or concern between meetings, it's great to be able to get in touch with others in the group. Establish a prayer chain in your group with a key contact person. Once that person is contacted, he or she will get in touch with the next person on the list and so on. Each person only needs to remember who he or she is to call. Contacting a key person in each small group can also be a great way to get prayer concerns out to the whole church or fellowship.

PRAYER CLOCK
Rob Stroud

Have each group member cut a circle from posterboard or cardstock. Each person should divide their circles into segments—one segment for each person in the group. Color each segment differently and write the name of one group member in each. In the center of each "clock" attach an arrow that will be turned once a day. The entire group can cover the designated person in prayer for that day. Your group can also add room on each "clock" segment for prayer requests or create blank segments as a reminder to pray for seekers.

PRAYER PARTNERS
Cindy Meyers

How can we draw near to God? How do we spur one another on toward love and good deeds? Through praying together (1 Thessalonians 5:17-18) and bearing one another's burdens (Galatians 6:1-2). Prayer partners:

- Describe specifically what the Lord has taught them and what they know the Lord is trying to teach them.

- Talk purposefully, avoiding a mere social session of aimless gabbing.

- Pray specifically for one another's needs, for plans and for common concerns.

- Pray purposefully, expecting God to act in their lives and willing to be used of God in answering their prayers.

- Pray habitually, looking to the Lord as a first response to situations rather than as a last resort.

- Pray for each other through the week and not just when together.

Prayer partners are not just "bowling buddies" who meet regularly to participate in an activity. A prayer partnership is not a new form of Christian dating. While engaged and married couples certainly should pray together, men and women who are not already committed to each other should probably not form a prayer partnership. A prayer partnership is not a substitute for one's personal relationship with the Lord.

Prayer partners are Christians who have committed themselves to an open and honest relationship. It is in some ways risky, but it is a risk that the Lord honors when two people become serious about meeting with him and growing together.

PRAYER TREE
Hallie Cowan

The prayer tree is made of paper or wood (be creative) which is hung on a wall or put in a stand so that paper leaves can be attached to it. Each leaf contains one prayer request and the date it was written. Each request must be specific so you can tell when God has answered the prayer. (Not "God bless my roommate," but "Find a ride home for Jim.")

Keep no more than two or three current requests per group member on leaves at one time. The group can agree together when and how to add leaves for concerns they all want to pray for. If you meet daily, you may want to keep the leaves in a central "leaf box." If you meet weekly, you could hand out leaves so one person can pray daily for each request. When a prayer is answered, add the leaf to the tree as a sign of God's provision and your thanksgiving. (If the answer is no, you can hang the leaf off to the side or under the tree.)

Groups report that when the first leaf goes up on the tree, there is real excitement and a desire to pray more. Then, as more and more leaves are added, the enthusiasm continues to grow! With a prayer tree you can see that God really does answer prayer!

PRAYER WALKS
Patty Pell

Divide into groups of two and three and walk around the campus or the community near a group member's home. As you walk, pray conversationally for the people who live and work in the buildings you pass, bless the houses and dorm rooms, pray for people you see. Listen for the prompting of the Holy Spirit to show you how to pray.

READ THE HEADLINES
Lisa Boegner

Cut out several headlines from various sections of a recent newspaper. Distribute the headlines to the group members. Then have each member come up with a spiritual application to the headline. For example, a headline that reads, "A Sure Victory, a Not So Sure Thing" could be associated with how everyone thought Goliath surely was going to beat David, but a sure victory in the eyes of the world is not so sure a thing especially when God is in control. It can also be used to remind us that when we try to do things on our own, without God, God may transform what we see as a sure victory into a learning experience.

RESPONSIVE READINGS
Hearing the Scripture read and giving a verbal response can be very power-

ful and can bring new insight. Many psalms are structured as liturgies of praise. For example, Psalm 136:1-6:

Give thanks to the Lord, for he is good.
His love endures forever.
Give thanks to the God of gods.
His love endures forever.
Give thanks to the Lord of lords;
His love endures forever.
to him who alone does great wonders,
His love endures forever.
who by his understanding made the heavens,
His love endures forever.
who spread out the earth upon the waters,
His love endures forever.

The psalm continues in this format for twenty-six verses. At the end you could add "Give thanks to the Lord, for _____ (something you are focusing on in your group)" with the response "His love endures forever." Other psalms can be used in this way simply by having the leader and the group alternate reading verses.

Responsive readings can also be found in hymnals and other worship resources. The "Litany of Worship" that follows is by Laura Urban, a member of a small group that was studying Joshua. You may want to create similar readings to celebrate and summarize what you are learning as a group. This litany can be read responsively, and individuals can fill in something personal in the blanks at the end.

It was the Lord our God himself who brought the Israelites out of Egypt.
Far be it from us to forsake the Lord to serve other gods!
It was the Lord our God himself who drive out other nations to give our spiritual forefathers the Promised Land.
Far be it from us to forsake the Lord to serve other gods!

It was the Lord our God himself who gave us a land in which we did not toil and cities we did not build, and we live in them and eat from vineyards and groves that we did not plant.

Far be it from us to forsake the Lord to serve other gods!

It was the Lord our God himself who forgave our rebellion and our sins and brought us from darkness into light.

Far be it from us to forsake the Lord to serve other gods!

It was the Lord our God himself who established his throne in heaven, and his kingdom rules over all.

Far be it from us to forsake the Lord to serve other gods!

It is the Lord our God himself who wraps himself in light as with a garment; he stretches out the heavens like a tent.

Far be it from us to forsake the Lord to serve other gods!

It was the Lord our God himself who set his love with those who fear him.

Far be it from us to forsake the Lord to serve other gods!

It was the Lord our God himself who sent Jesus to be the priest to offer for all time one sacrifice for sins and who sits at the right hand of God.

Far be it from us to forsake the Lord to serve other gods!

It was the Lord our God himself who _____.

Far be it from us to forsake the Lord to serve other gods!

WE TOO WILL SERVE THE LORD, BECAUSE HE IS OUR GOD.

(Based on Joshua 24; Psalms 103—104; Hebrews 9—10)

RETREAT TOGETHER

Cindy Bunch

A weekend retreat devoted to times of solitude and times of teaching, study and group discussion can be a powerful bonding experience for your group. It is a great way to help people jumpstart their devotional lives and perhaps discover a new spiritual discipline. A great resource for building a retreat is *Quiet Places* by Jane Rubietta. It offers retreat material on a variety of topics. Another excellent resource for group retreats is the Spiritual Disciplines Bible Study Series by Jan Johnson. Pick one of the guides in the series, such as *Solitude and Silence,* and work through it over a weekend.

REVIVAL PRAYER

Dave Bryant (Taken from "An Amazing Prayer Movement Signals Hope for World Revival," World Evangelization, *September/October 1994, p. 9)*

This is a fifteen-minute daily discipline of revival prayer.

- Rejoice (one minute)—praise God for what he has done, is doing and is getting ready to do in world revival.

- Review (five minutes)—read books, magazines, other literature and, most of all, the Scriptures to learn all you can about the nature of revival, its impact on missions and its current manifestation around the world.

- Repent (one minute)—confess to God on your behalf, and on behalf of the whole church, the specific ways in which we are hindering world revival.

- Resist (one minute)—target prayer on those points where Satan is attempting to undermine the life and mission of the church.

- Request (five minutes)—drawing from the vast reservoir of biblical promises, intercede for full revival in the church—both your own and the international church.

- Recommit (one minute)—reflect on all that you have learned from the Lord and all that you have said to him, and commit yourself back to him to be used in answer to your prayers.

- Record (one minute)—keep a journal to record whatever you sense God has said to you. What new understandings has he given you of revival? What new directions has he given for prayer? How has he encouraged you to influence others?

SILENT REFLECTION

Mary Hays

The leader introduces each time of silent reflection with phrases like "Reflect on the past twenty-four hours and pray silently." "Thank God for what he has done in these hours." "Praise God for what you have seen of his character in these hours." "Confess things you've done to separate yourself from God." "Pray for the person on your right . . . on your left."

STUDY PRAYER

Small Group Network

Look at different ways to pray as shown in Scripture: raising hands, kneeling, lying prostrate. Do a study on the book of Acts with special emphasis on prayer. Use this time to emphasize prayer in the group, putting into practice what you are learning together.

TAKE OUT THE GARBAGE

Lisa Boegner

For this you need several sheets of paper and a garbage bag. Hand out the pieces of paper and have everyone write some "sin" in their life that they want to get rid of. Then have someone pray. Next, have each person wad up the piece of paper and throw it in the garbage bag to symbolize getting rid of the trash in our life.

TEMPERATURE READING

Bob Wolnicak (From "Why Pray Together," Student Leadership, Fall 1993, p. 17)

To gauge how you are doing with prayer as a group, discuss how people are feeling about prayer. What do they know about it? How does it affect them? Ask if anyone has a prayer experience they'd like to talk about. Ask what part members would like prayer to play in your group. Then study a passage about prayer such as Matthew 6:5-15; Mark 1:35-39; Luke 11:1-13; John 17 or Nehemiah 1.

VICTORY PRAYER
Charles Stanley

In his book *The Wonderful Spirit-Filled Life* Charles Stanley encourages us to claim God's promise of victory before we face predictable battles as well as in the midst of them. This prayer can encourage group members who are struggling with temptation and complement studies dealing with spiritual battles.

> Lord, I claim victory right now over the giant of _____. I recognize that this giant is coming against the Christ in me. Just as You defeated this giant when You walked on this earth, you can defeat it through me now, for You are my life. I trust You to produce peace and self-control through me. When the pressure comes, remind me that the battle is Yours. Amen.

WISH PRAYER
Elsie Larsen (From Daily Guideposts 1994, *p. 201.)*

In Isaiah 65:24 we read "Before they call I will answer; / while they are still speaking I will hear." God knows our wishes—what we hope for—before we even realize we should pray for them. Since I discovered what can happen when I wish something good for someone, wishing has become fun for me. Every greeting card I send is really a wish and a prayer. Throughout the day, as I see a need, I offer wishes for others like good thoughts blown their way. The rest I leave to God. He understands and answers.

Your group could offer "wish prayers" for one another as a way of showing understanding and offering encouragement. It will be exciting to see what God does as you dream of the Lord's best for one another.

WORSHIP POSTER
Nina Thiel

Get a large posterboard or five-foot piece of butcher paper. Bring colored markers, magazines, scissors and glue. Have everyone gather around and make a visual representation of praise to God, each on their own "corner" of the poster. They can make a collage, draw a picture, write a verse and so on. Put it up on the wall when everyone's done.

WRITE

Sometimes it is helpful to collect our thoughts and write them down. Think over the last day or two. List things for which you are thankful. Share your list with the group. Have members lead in prayer as they praise God with what they have written. Write letters of gratitude to God; share parts of them; pray them conversationally back to God.

Creative writing can also be a help in worship. Give group members time to write a poem, song or psalm. Read them to each other, using them as an introduction to worship.

BOOKS AND BIBLE STUDIES ON WORSHIP AND PRAYER

Beckwith, Paul, Hughes Huffman, and Mark Hunt, eds. *Hymns II.* Downers Grove, Ill.: InterVarsity Press, 1976. A collection of hymns—some old, some new. Hymns II is packed full of praise and honor to God. Guitar chords are given.

Companion Songbook for Prayer and Worship for Small Groups. Wholehearted Worship, P. O. Box 850242, Mobile, AL 36685 (205) 660-7288.

Foster, Richard. *Celebration of Discipline.* San Francisco: Harper & Row, 1978. Insightful writing on twelve key spiritual disciplines.

——. *Prayer: Finding the Heart's True Home.* San Francisco: Harper & Row, 1992. Looks at what prayer is and how it works in our lives.

Foster, Richard, and James Bryan Smith. *Devotional Classics.* San Francisco: Harper & Row, 1990. Readings from writers like Bernard of Clairvaux, Augustine and C. S. Lewis, with Bible passages and discussion questions.

Gregg, Doug, and Mike Flynn. *Inner Healing.* Downers Grove, Ill.: InterVarsity Press, 1993. Focuses on healing prayer.

Hallesby, O. *Prayer.* Minneapolis, Minn.: Augsburg, 1959. Discusses our motivation for prayer and what God wants to teach us about himself through prayer.

Huggett, Joyce. *The Joy of Listening to God.* Downers Grove, Ill.: InterVarsity Press, 1986. Focuses on hearing God in prayer and silence.

Integrity Music, Inc. P.O. Box 5205, Clifton, NJ 05015-9785. Instrumental and vocal tapes, CDs, and printed music for worship.

Johnson, Jan. Spiritual Disciplines Bible Studies. Downers Grove, Ill.: InterVarsity Press, 2003. Use these guides as a way of focusing Bible studies on worship, or mix in selected ideas or exercises to any small group session.

Johnstone, Patrick. *Operation World.* 5th edition. Grand Rapids, Mich.: Zondervan, 1993. A daily guide to praying for the world with facts about missions in every part of the world.

Mains, Karen. *The God Hunt.* Downers Grove, Ill.: InterVarsity Press, 2003. Helps us become more aware of how God works daily in our lives.

Marshall, Catherine. "Prayer of Relinquishment." *Guideposts*, March 1993, reprinted from October 1960. Deals with the question of unanswered prayer and giving up our will for God's will.

Packer, J. I. *Knowing God.* Downers Grove, Ill.: InterVarsity Press, 1973. Packer asks: What were we made for? What aim should we set in life? What is the best thing in life? What in us gives God the most pleasure? The answer to all these questions is to know God. As Packer teaches us about God we are led to worship. Focus on the section "Behold Your God."

———. *Meeting God.* A LifeGuide® Bible Study. Downers Grove, Ill.: InterVarsity Press, 1986. Twelve inductive Bible studies focusing on the character of God.

Patterson, Ben. *Worship.* A Christian Basics Bible Study. Downers Grove, Ill.: InterVarsity Press, 1994. Six inductive studies on the biblical basis of worship.

Peace, Richard. *Spiritual Journaling.* Colorado Springs: NavPress, 1995. A resource for groups who want to learn to journal together. With individual exercises, group discussion questions and Bible studies.

Peterson, Eugene. *Answering God: The Psalms as Tools for Prayer.* San Francisco: Harper & Row, 1989.

Piper, John. *The Pleasures of God.* Portland, Ore.: Multnomah, 1991. In chapter eight, "The Pleasure of God in the Prayers of the Upright," Piper emphasizes that it is not we who meet God's needs in prayer but God who meets our needs: "The way to *please* God is to come to him to get and not to give. . . . He is most glorified in us when we are most satisfied in him" (p. 216).

Postema, Don. *Space for God.* Grand Rapids: CRC Publications, 1983.

Rinker, Rosalind. *Learning Conversational Prayer.* Collegeville, Minn.: Liturgical Press, 1992.

Ryan, Dale, and Juanita. *Recovering from Distorted Images of God.* Life Recovery Guides. Downers Grove, Ill.: InterVarsity Press, 1990. An inductive Bible study that leads people to consider how their view of God has been distorted by family and church experiences and to have their vision transformed by Scripture.

Tozer, A. W. *The Knowledge of the Holy.* New York: Harper & Row, 1978. "Written for plain persons whose hearts stir them up to seek after God Himself." Each chapter begins with a prayer and ends with a verse. The chapters are designed to help us appreciate God, especially his majesty and holiness.

Trevethan, Thomas L. *The Beauty of God's Holiness.* Downers Grove, Ill.: InterVarsity Press, 1995. In a book that is at once a manifesto and a devotional guide, the author vividly reminds us that holiness is an essential characteristic of the biblical Lord. He carefully describes the true shape of God's majesty, then devotes several chapters to life before the Holy One—living as if God really is the center of all creation.

Wallace, Daniel B. "Who's Afraid of the Holy Spirit?" *Christianity Today,* September 12, 1994, pp. 35-38. A skeptical Dallas Theological Seminary professor explores the charismatic movement and discovers anew how God works in the world today.

Webber, Robert. *Worship Is a Verb.* Nashville: Star Song, 1992. Defines worship as an active expression of the Christian faith as a community.

_____. *Worship Old & New.* Grand Rapids: Zondervan, 1994. Shows how the traditions of the early church can be applied in meaningful ways to worship today.

White, John. *Daring to Draw Near.* Downers Grove, Ill.: InterVarsity Press, 1977. White examines ten prayers from the Bible and helps us learn about prayer, God and those praying.

PART THREE

STUDY

Keeping the Bible at the heart of what you do together will be
critical to growing in Christ together. There are lots of creative
ways to explore God's Word together that will draw out the truth
and help you remember what you are learning. Here are some
ideas for creative Bible study.

ACTING OUT THE TEXT

Kelle Ashton

When you are studying a Gospel or the book of Acts, instead of reading the passage have each person take a different part. Act out the passage or read it dramatically. Then discuss how each person felt and the insights they gained from acting instead of reading.

APPLICATION QUESTIONS FOR BIBLE STUDY

Mike Shepherd

Application—putting truth into practice—is one of the hardest things to integrate into your Bible study. The following table provides some application questions to consider when preparing a Bible study.

Application Questions

	People's need/problems	God's action/solution	People's response/obedience
T H E N	Who needed help? What was going on? What was the problem?	How did God react? What did God do? What did God want the people to do?	How did the people receive God's message? How did the people respond to God's solution? How did God want the people to respond?
N O W	Who do I identify with? What tension, need, conflict or problem sounds familiar? How are the people in this story like us?	What is God's answer to this question today? What is God's solution to our problem? What is God doing now?	How does God want people to receive his message? How does God want us to react? How should people put this truth into practice?
M E	How am I facing a similar problem in my life? How are the people in the passage like me? What in this passage makes me feel uneasy or gives me a sense of conviction?	What does God want to do in my life now? How is God involved with me? What kind of person does God want me to become?	In what area of my life do I need to be obedient to God? What can I do to become the person God wants me to be? What specific steps should I take this week?

APPLY THE WORD
Bill Clark

One way to be sure you don't miss the important step of application is to study a Scripture passage one week and then focus on applying the passage the following week. For example, after studying the lifestyle of the early church as depicted in Acts 2, one small group was convicted by the level of care the new believers had for each other's practical needs. The group decorated an old box, brought it to their IVCF large group meeting and encouraged the fellowship that if anyone had a need to make it known. Week after week, requests are placed in the box, and week after week the small group mobilizes the chapter to help meet those needs. The entire fellowship has been challenged by this bold application of Scripture and encouraged to see God active in making provisions for these needs.

ASSIGN HOMEWORK
Jeff Grant

Doing homework creates a readiness to respond, thoughtful participation and an eagerness to enjoy. Here are some homework assignments you can take on between group meetings:

- Do a little extra reading. Reread your favorite Gospel, because there's no better example of what, how and who we should be than Christ himself. He is known, even by non-Christian and nonreligious people, as the greatest teacher of all time, so it certainly couldn't hurt to take some more instruction from the Master. Dig into a few of Paul's letters—they are packed with sound advice and sage criticisms that will help us maintain the course. Marvel again at the beginning of the world in Genesis; take a tour of some of God's miracles and promises; refamiliarize yourself with the passion of the prophets. Maybe even take another crack at the revelation of the end times, so that we might better be ready.

- We all probably need to do some research. Buy a current concordance, which better explains some complex truths of Scriptures. Interview some older, wiser people in your church and small group. Learn the history of the Holy Land. Surf the Web for books. In short, root yourself in the truths of God. A plant is only as healthy as its core, its structure.

- Write your own testimony, not necessarily to be shared word-for-word in a later encounter but rather to clarify in your mind that which has been true of God's influence on your life, in order to better lead a friend to a saving knowledge of Jesus Christ. It seems odd that anyone would voluntarily write out what they already know, but again, homework establishes foundational truths, upon which bigger and better things might be built.

- Small group time is great, but find a homework group too, even of one other person. You'll find in that intimacy an accountability to work harder on Jesus' lessons.

BIBLE CHARADES
Irma Hider

Put the names of books in the Bible into a hat for a game of charades. Or use this as a summary of the book or topic the group has been studying. You might want to ask the group members to write down the topics to be acted out.

COLLAGES
Sue Sage

This is a creative way to express almost any idea that you have been focusing on—a Scripture passage, an element of your community life, something that is happening on your campus, answers to prayer. All you need are scissors, glue, magazines and paper. Have each person explain their collage, and you will learn a lot about him or her!

CONFERENCES

Attend a conference oriented toward small groups and Bible study such as the annual Willow Creek Association small group conference <www .willowcreek.com> or the Bible & Life conference sponsored by InterVarsity Christian Fellowship. Bible & Life is an excellent resource for small group leaders because it takes them through the basics of leading in the sequence of three weekends as follows.

- Level 1: The Joy of Following Jesus—the basics of spiritual formation and friendship evangelism

- Level 2: The Joy of Bible Discovery—how to study the Bible for yourself and how to prepare and lead studies

- Level 3: The Joy of Growing Together—vision and tools for disciple-making

Prayerfully support each other throughout the event, and hold one another accountable for personal commitments made at the conference. Afterward, talk about it over pizza at someone's home.

CONTRASTS

Margaret Parker (Adapted from "Exploring Contrasts," Student Leadership, Spring 1990, p. 11.)

God has inspired the biblical writers to present vivid contrasts—light versus darkness, life versus death, love verses alienation—to highlight the crucial choices before us and help us choose rightly. You can help group members experience the persuasive, life-changing power of God's Word by focusing their attention on the contrasts in Scripture. For example, with the parable of the prodigal son (Luke 15:11-32) ask people to list every contrast they can find in the passage. Then have them choose one area of contrast and explore it more fully. Be sure people understand that they can use their imaginations to flesh out the various elements of the contrast.

Suppose your group explores the differences between the life the prodigal son led in the far country and the life he found waiting at home. As they imagine what the prodigal must have experienced, they will find the parable draws a sharp contrast between two kinds of partying. The phrases "squandered his wealth in wild living" (v. 13) and "no one gave him anything" (v. 16) suggest that in the far country the prodigal tried desperately to buy fun and friends, but instead found only fleeting, dehumanizing pleasures followed by painful disillusionment and abandonment. How different from the homecoming party that greeted his return, where real pleasures (hugs and kisses, new clothes, a great feast, music and dancing) were given freely to the prodigal as expressions of his father's love for him, a love that nothing he had done could ever cancel out. These contrasts can lead to the personal application that our choice is not between partying and God but between joyful, lasting fellowship and illusory fun.

DAILY DISCOVERY

This system for personal inductive Bible study helps you find the central truth in a passage and build that truth into your life. Use this approach for a while, then share it with a friend! To get the most from this study you need (1) a version of the Bible with paragraphs (go to <www.biblegateway.net> and print out the portion you want to study) and (2) a notebook for writing down your findings.

- When you open God's Word, expect to meet with him and to learn something about him. Expect to find more of who he is and what he wants you to be like. If you approach the Bible open to be changed by what you find there, you'll grow in a wonderful way to understand God and his ways.

- Each day as you begin, open your heart to the teaching of the Holy Spirit; ask him to give you understanding and to help you think and act in God's ways.

- As you conclude a day's study, apply to your life one truth God has shown you as you relate to him.

- Do as much of a step as is comfortable each day.

Step 1. Book Overview

Read it, if it's brief. If it's long, skim it. If it's a narrative, jot down a fact about one or two of the main characters; list a few major events. If it's a letter, note a few facts about the writer and those being addressed. If it's another kind of literature, list some facts that impress you.

Write down a few of your major impressions of the book.

What helps do you think you'll get for your life from this book? Write down one or two and ask the Lord to move in your life in these ways.

Step 2. The Book (continued)

Look through the book to find which chapters can be most naturally grouped together, either by main characters, by events or by geography. On a simple chart, show the two or three or four major divisions of the book, the natural groups of chapters. Give each division a short title.

What seems to be the main theme of the book? Write it in a short sentence over your chart.

How does that theme apply to you personally? In what part of your life do you need to act on that truth? Write down a specific way you can begin to do that and ask the Lord to strengthen you in it.

Step 3. Chapter or Part of a Chapter

(If your version of the Bible has many short paragraphs, you can group them into thought-units and treat each unit as you would a paragraph.)

Make a list of facts that you observe in the chapter (or part). Note who, when, what, where and how. Also note any interesting things about people, places, situations, atmosphere. Include things that are emphasized, like words that are repeated or contrasted. To cover a passage, make just a few observations on each paragraph.

Write down your major impressions of the passage. What hits you from this passage?

What does this passage teach about the Lord? What difference does it make to you that he is like this? Take some time to praise him.

Step 4. The Chapter or Part (continued)

Choose a short title for each paragraph.

What connections can you find between paragraphs? Look for a few, such as repeated words, similarities, contrasts, cause and effect. What significance or meaning do you find in each of these connections? Jot down the meanings.

Then, look at the meanings, connections and facts, and ask yourself, *What is the main thing going on in this passage?* In other words, what is the central truth this passage is teaching? Write that truth in a sentence.

What is the main thing the Lord is saying to me through this passage? Here are some possibilities. Select just one.

- Something to obey or an example to follow or avoid? What is it exactly? How can I soon practice it?

- A truth about the Lord I can rejoice in? In what part of my life is this truth especially encouraging?

- A promise I can take for a situation I'm in? Are there conditions in the promise that I need to fulfill? What are they? What does the Lord say he'll do? (Memorizing the promise will help in the days ahead.)

Step 5. The Next Chapter or Part

Continue as in step 3 then proceed as in step 4. Move along at your own pace.

Step 6. The Theme

When you finish studying the chapters, notice how their main truths connect with each other. As you connect these main truths, you are beginning to put together the teaching of the Bible. See if from these you can write the theme of the book in a sentence. How does it fit with the theme you saw at first? Share these with a Christian friend or group studying the same book. See how your theme compares with that in a Bible handbook.

DISCUSSION QUESTIONS

Jim Nyquist and Jack Kuhatschek (originally published in Leading Bible Discussions)

Sometimes a question which looks good on paper may not work in a group. Likewise, some seemingly ordinary questions may do an excellent job of generating discussion. It is a good idea, then, to evaluate your questions again at the end of the study.

The table on pages 107-8 examines questions that might flow out of a discussion of Luke 4:38-39: "Jesus left the synagogue and went to the home of Simon. Now Simon's mother-in-law was suffering from a high fever, and they asked Jesus to help her. So he bent over her and rebuked the fever, and it left her: she got up at once and began to wait on them."

Evaluating Questions

Observation Questions	*Evaluation*
1a. Who are the characters in this incident?	1a. This forces the group to look at the entire section. But it might better be put in simpler terms, as in 1b.
1b. Who are the people in this story?	1b. A clearer way of putting 1a.
1c. Describe the people in this story.	1c. The word *describe* stimulates a more extensive searching of the text than the simple word *who* and should encourage broader discussion.
2a. Was Simon's mother-in-law ill?	2a. This one-word answer, yes, may be considered too simple and obvious. It doesn't provoke much thought.
2b. What happened to the fever?	2b. Same problems as question 2a.
2c. What did each person in the story do?	2c. Stimulates searching of the text and allows several members to respond.
3a. How did Jesus affect the different people in this story?	3a. This question highlights Jesus as the center of the story, and fits in with the purpose of Luke, the author.
3b. What does this story teach us about Jesus?	3b. More comprehensive than 3a and allows the group to think about any aspect of Jesus that the story covers.

Interpretation Questions	*Evaluation*
4a. What does this story teach us about faith?	4a. In a beginning group, this question may not be easily grasped.
4b. What can we learn from the faith of those who asked Jesus to help the woman?	4b. This focuses attention on one particular aspect of the story and may keep the discussion from rambling.
5a. How does Jesus' healing reveal his authority?	5a. This simple question leads into some basic issues that Luke, the author, speaks about frequently.
5b. What are the implications of Jesus' power over sickness?	5b. For a more advanced group, this kind of question may be stimulating. A beginning group may find 5c better.
5c. Discuss how this episode with Jesus might have affected the household of Simon.	5c. The word *discuss* encourages a wide-ranging exploration of the subject, and could lead to unprofitable speculation if the leader is not alert.
6a. Imagine that you are the mother-in-law of Simon (a) when Jesus arrived and (b)	6a. The leader could ask one person to respond to both parts or have two people respond to one

when you were healed.
6b. What can we learn about healing from this story?

part each.
6b. Don't include too many speculative lessons.

Application Questions

7a. Let's discuss how Jesus affects our ability and desire to serve.

7b. Do we believe Jesus can help people today? In what ways?

7c. Do we believe that Jesus actually performed a miracle of healing as this story depicts? If not, why not?

7d. Have you asked Jesus to enter your home? Life? Why haven't we done so?

Evaluation

7a. Not very stimulating. It needs to be cast as a question.

7b. This question not only addresses the ability of Jesus, but our faith and confidence in him. If your group has people in it who are not Christians, a better question could be 7c.

7c. For those who have not yet been able to build much confidence in Jesus, this question could provide a context for growth.

7d. This type of application question can be very threatening to some individuals. But if the climate of the study is loving, it is often surprising how open the discussion following this straightforward type of question can be.

EMOTIONAL IMPACT

Margaret Parker (Adapted from "Recapturing the Bible's Emotional Impact," Student Leadership, *Winter 1988, p. 13.)*

The Bible is personal communication, God speaking to us through the voices of people in history. As a leader, you can help group members be sensitive to the emotional content of the passages they study. One way to foster this sensitivity is to suggest that they listen for tones of voice and visualize facial expressions as they read God's Word. Or have a group member read dramatically as they feel its author would have spoken it. Have the rest of the group imagine they are members of the original audience hearing the message for the first time and talk about how they would have responded. This approach works well with the poetry in the Bible, particularly Psalms and the Prophets (see, for example, Isaiah 1:2; 13; 18). The Epistles, too, often convey emotions (see Galatians 4:9-11). Strong emotional currents also underlie the historical narratives in Scripture (see Luke 7:36-50).

EXPERIENCE

Each of us has ways in which God has been working in us. We also have had different experiences in dealing with doubt, pain, death, joy, love and so on. Share these experiences with each other so others can benefit and grow from one another's experience. Remember that one person's experience is not descriptive of what every other person's experience will be or should be. God meets us as individuals. This time is to help us encourage one another, not prescribe cures.

HELP PEOPLE LEARN

Mike Shepherd

We remember best what we discover ourselves! Here are some keys to helping your group members learn.

- People learn better when they respond actively. Ask the group to analyze a case study or tell the biblical story in their own words.

- People learn better when the truth is presented in a variety of ways. Read it, then show it, then play it.

- People learn better when they use one or more of their senses. This could involve hearing, seeing, touching, smelling and even tasting.

- People learn better when they repeat what they learn. Ask people to preview, review, summarize, brainstorm and report.

- People learn better when they move from the simple to the complex. Illustrate with stories and well-known facts and ideas.

- People learn better when truth is presented in an organized manner. Use an outline, present orally or visually the transition from point to point, set up the Bible discussion topic clearly, and summarize main points.

- People learn better when they feel free to respond. Use a conversational tone, include humor, tell personal experiences, begin with an icebreaker, and invite people to share.

INTEGRATE YOUR ICEBREAKER

Dan Lentz

How do we create a life-changing intersection between sharing our own life experiences and studying God's Word? How can we steer those icebreaker questions and responses so they help people make the intersection between the truth about their lives and the truth about God?

One option is to intentionally select an icebreaker that connects with the biblical truth you hope to talk about during your group meeting. Then during your Bible study, ask follow-up questions that connect the icebreaker to the truth of the Scripture you are discussing.

Jesus was a master at using this technique in his teaching. He started with questions about common life and moved to questions about life transformation (see the table on page 111).

JESUS' FAMILY

Irma Hider

This is a great way to begin studying Matthew or any of the Gospels. Don't tell the group that this is about the genealogy of Jesus. Give individuals or pairs different Scriptures to look up surrounding one of the following key characters. (How many you use depends on how many people are in the group.) They are responsible for reporting back to the group in three to four minutes what they learned about their character.

- Rahab (Joshua 2:1-24; 6:20-25; Hebrews 11:31; James 2:25)
- Jesse (1 Samuel 16:1-13)
- Naomi, Ruth, Boaz (Ruth 1:1-22; 2:11-12; 4:13-22)
- Judah, Tamar, Perez (Genesis 38:1-19)
- Moab (Genesis 19:30-38)
- David (2 Samuel 11:1-27; 12:15-18)
- Abraham (Genesis 12:1, 11-13; 16:3-15; 21:1-3)
- Isaac, Jacob (Genesis 25:19-26; Hebrews 11:8-10)

Jesus' Icebreakers and Follow-Up Questions

Scripture Reference	Jesus' Icebreaker	Jesus' Follow-Up Truth Questions
Matthew 20:21 (Jesus talking to James, John and their mother)	"What is it that you want to have most?" Modern paraphrase: What goals do you have for your life?	"Can you drink the cup I am going to drink?" Modern paraphrase: Do you really want what God wants? And have you counted the cost?
Matthew 16:28 (Jesus talking to the Twelve)	"Who do other people say the Son of Man is?" Modern paraphrase: What spiritually-related news headline has gotten your attention recently?	"Who do you say I am?" Modern paraphrase: Is the "word on the street" and the world influencing you more than God is influencing you? Who is Jesus becoming to you?
Mark 6:38 (Jesus talking to the Twelve before feeding the five thousand)	"How many loaves of bread do you have?" Modern paraphrase: Do you ever feel like there are things you should do but lack the resources to accomplish them?	"Do you believe I can feed my people?" Modern paraphrase: Is your faith grounded in the quantity of physical resources you have or in God's provision?
Luke 24:17 (Jesus talking with two followers along the road to Emmaus)	"What are you discussing together as you walk along?" Modern paraphrase: What difficult conversation have you had recently?	"Did not the Christ have to suffer these things and then enter his glory?" Modern paraphrase: Can you see how the life trials and problems you have described are opportunities for God to work out his glorious plan in your life?
Luke 10:26 (Jesus talking to a group of seekers)	"What is written in the Law?" Modern paraphrase: What absolute truth have you been convicted of recently?	"How do you read it?" Modern paraphrase: What is God telling you to do because of knowing this truth?

As people tell what they learned (in no particular order) try to find some ties between the family, personal and spiritual histories of the characters. By the end you will have read about incest, murder, adultery, a prostitute and the promises of God. After you are done with this, read the genealogy of Jesus (Matthew 1:1-17). By this time some members of the group will have started to catch on. The point is to see that Jesus' family is made up of broken, sinful people, and we are each descendants of Christ. In the same way he accepted his ancestors and the roots from which he came, he also accepts each of us as members of his family no matter what sinfulness may be a part of our past. Reflect on Romans 8:14-17 and Galatians 3:29 and offer prayers of thanksgiving that we are children of God and heirs with Christ.

MAKE BIBLE STUDY MORE INTERACTIVE
James M. Kovach

Write down the Scripture verses you intend to use on small strips of "sticky notes," and give one or more to each person in the group to look up and read. They won't feel singled out but will feel a part of a team effort. (Be sensitive to those you know who don't like to read in public.)

Use a flip-chart to record responses to a discussion question. As you go around the room, the chart provides group members with a visual aid that may jog their mind for an answer.

MAKE USE OF DRAMA
Mike Shepherd

The Jewish culture of Jesus' time was quite used to reenactment of history. Instead of reading about the past, they relived it—their festivals and feasts often took on a life of their own. Jesus understood the importance of reenactment in his culture, and he used it at the inauguration of his baptism and the Lord's Supper, when driving the money-changers out of the temple, and in his dramatic entry into Jerusalem on a donkey as people waved palm branches.

How can you create a dramatic experience to communicate truth? Is there a place or event your group can experience together to gain a better understanding of truth?

MAKE USE OF OBJECTS
Mike Shepherd

Jesus was a close observer of nature and made considerable use of natural objects and symbols in his teaching, including the sun, rain, a vine, branches, a fig tree, a mustard seed, an ear of corn, wheat, tares, sparrows, ravens, eagles, vipers, oxen, foxes, dogs, sheep, goats, light and soil. Other symbolic images from Jesus' teaching and parables include Caesar's coin, a water pot, a skin of wine, a lamp, a bushel measure, the widow's mite, a farmer sowing seed, fishing, constructing a house and going to war. His actions of placing a child in the center of the group and washing his disciples feet were also symbolic.

Nothing escaped Jesus' eye. He used current events and daily chores to make truth come alive. How can we use the elements of nature and other objects around us to illustrate truth?

MEMORIZE SCRIPTURE
Hold each other accountable to committing Scripture to memory, perhaps working with prayer partners. Learn a psalm a month. Memorize one verse or passage from the book you are studying.

MOVIE CLIPS
For a powerful and gripping opening to your Bible study, watch a movie clip together to kick off the discussion. Pick a brief segment (five minutes or so) that will relate to what you are discussing. One approach would be to contrast the world's view with a Christian view. Rick Richardson's series Groups Investigating God has some great ideas for using movie clips with Bible study.

PLAN THE YEAR
Bible study will probably be the main source of nurture for your group. But don't let your creativity in planning stop there. Vary the kind of study you do over a period of time. Include an inductive study on a particular topic of interest, a character study, a manuscript study, a study of an Old Testament book, and a study of a New Testament book. You may want to intermix

other ideas (like watching and discussing a DVD together one week) with Bible study series for a different focus for a week or two.

PORTFOLIO OF PROMISES

Keith D. Wright

By recording how the Lord speaks through his Word in the midst of specific circumstances, we acquire a permanent record of God's faithfulness. Use some small group meetings to build a "Portfolio of Promises" from the Scriptures together.

Divide a notebook into five sections and title them Power, Person, Promises, Presence and Purposes. As you learn about God's character and ways from your Bible reading, discuss and record insights in the appropriate section.

- *Power.* When faced with situations that seem impossible, we need reminders of God's sufficient and sustaining power. This section is for recording how God reveals his power both in Scripture and in the events of your life.

- *Person.* As we meet Christ in the pages of the Word, we form a cumulative knowledge of his nature. By recording insights and revelations about the Savior, you will develop a testimony of a growing, intimate relationship.

- *Promises.* What benefits does God offer to those who live for him? A record of his promises can keep you motivated and focused.

- *Presence.* Sometimes God's presence seems elusive. Keep a record of how God reveals himself to you. This can sustain your faith at times when God seems distant.

- *Purposes.* God's plans often differ from the messages that bombard us daily. Recording God's revealed purposes for living can help you stay on the path God has prepared for you.

QUIET TIMES

Encourage one another to do quiet times by using the Daily Discovery system (see p. 104). You may also want to work through the quiet times in a Spiritual Encounter Guide, such as *Entering God's Presence*, or in Stephen Eyre's *Drawing Close to God* and follow his suggestions for discussing your quiet time experiences in a group. Or use the daily quiet times in the *Quiet Time Bible* to prepare for the book you are studying in your small group.

SET THE BAR FOR GREAT BIBLE DISCUSSION
Mike Shepherd

- Ask questions that require more than a yes-or-no answer.
- Ask thought-provoking questions.
- Ask clear, short questions. Make them concise.
- Don't ask rhetorical questions.
- Don't ask trick questions.
- Don't ask questions that would insult or embarrass someone.
- Move from simple questions to complex.
- Move from general questions to specific.
- Allow time for persons to respond.
- Don't use questions that have only one answer ("What I was really looking for was . . .").
- Listen to the answer. Look at the person. Don't be thinking about what you are doing next or looking down at your lesson.
- Acknowledge the response ("Thank you." "That's good!").
- Show interest in what the person is saying.
- Give everyone a copy of your questions when you begin the lesson. Use a handout or three-by-five cards.
- Assign questions to subgroups of four for greater discussion and participation.

- Don't be afraid to say, "I don't know. What do you think?"

- Rephrase the answer: "Are you saying . . . ?"

- Summarize the discussion.

- Don't be afraid to let a question sit there in silence. Use the pregnant pause.

Value the contribution of those in your group, and they will respond.

SPIRITUAL CHALLENGE CARDS
Jeff Howell

To create spiritual challenge cards, you will need several index cards for each group member. On one side of each card, each person should write a challenging question that focuses on an area of spiritual growth for them. On the other side of the card, they should place a symbol to indicate one of three areas of spiritual growth. The three suggested categories are head, heart and hand:

- *Head.* Questions on these cards focus on things that we learn. In order to grow spiritually we need to make an effort to understand what God is telling us in his Word.

- *Heart.* Questions on this card relate to active application of what God is revealing to us in our heart, so that we are developing Christlike character.

- *Hand:* Questions having to do with the hand encourage us to love others as God loves us.

There are several ways to use the cards in your group, depending on the size and member participation. One way is to have several people in turn pick a card, read the question aloud and then answer it from their own current experiences. Another way is to invite the whole group to discuss each question. You could make the spiritual challenge cards a regular part of each meeting to help people grow in accountability with one another. You will be rewarded in learning from others how God has taught them to draw closer to him.

STEP INTO SCRIPTURE

Nairy Ohanian

This activity expands our knowledge of biblical characters and godly attributes, as well as our understanding of one another. Ask the group who their favorite biblical heroes and heroines are. Have them either draw this character as they imagine them to be or simply write the name of the person on paper. Next to each drawing or name, have everyone write what they respect about the person. Have each person talk about how they relate to this person and in what ways they want to be like the person. Have the members in the group pray for each other, specifically asking God to fill them with the desired qualities of their Bible hero or heroine.

TANGENT BALL

This idea is for a group whose members are pretty comfortable with each other, probably in the live-it-up phase. At the beginning of the study give one member a Nerf ball (or a wad of paper). During the Bible discussion, if another member goes off on a tangent, the holder of the ball throws it at that person. That person is then in charge of the ball. This is a good way to give control of the study to the group members, and it takes the burden of keeping the study on track off the leader. The tangent ball should not be used when someone is talking about his or her life, a deep concern or a prayer request.

TRAINING

Train your group to do inductive Bible study using *Transforming Bible Study* by Bob Grahmann. Grow in your ability to lead using study guides by working through *How to Lead a LifeGuide Bible Study*. Rotate leadership among those you are training. Read through *The Big Book on Small Groups* or *Small Group Leaders' Handbook* with one or two potential leaders in the group.

USE BIBLE STUDY GUIDES

InterVarsity Press

Here are some different courses of study, from the LifeGuide Bible Study series, you might consider for your group. Some of these series are for specialized groups, and others are appropriate for everyone. Each series is designed to take less than a year.

Seeker Studies

Choose one of the following three guides.

- *Encountering Jesus*, 8 studies by Douglas Connelly
- *Jesus the Reason*, 11 studies by James W. Sire
- *Meeting Jesus*, 13 studies by Leighton Ford

Follow it with one of these studies of the Gospels.

- *Mark*, 20 studies by James W. Hoover
- *Luke*, 26 studies by Ada Lum

Finish the year with *Parables*, 12 studies by John White.

Outreach

- *Spiritual Gifts*, 12 studies by Charles and Anne Hummel
- *Evangelism*, 12 studies by Becky Pippert and Ruth Siemens
- *Loving Justice*, 12 studies by Bob and Carol Hunter
- *Missions*, 9 studies by Paul Borthwick

Singles

- *Singleness*, 10 studies by Ruth Goring
- *Friendship*, 12 studies by Carolyn Nystrom
- *Love*, 9 studies by Phyllis Le Peau

Pick a great Bible book to finish the series.

Women's Groups

- *Woman of God*, 10 studies by Cindy Bunch
- *Women of the New Testament*, 10 studies by Phyllis Le Peau

- *Women of the Old Testament,* 12 studies by Gladys Hunt
- *Esther,* 9 studies by Patty Pell

Christian Doctrine

- *Christian Beliefs,* 12 studies by Stephen D. Eyre
- *Meeting God,* 12 studies by J. I. Packer
- *Meeting Jesus,* 13 studies by Leighton Ford
- *Meeting the Spirit,* 10 studies by Douglas Connelly

Small Group Starter

- *Christian Community,* 10 studies by Rob Suggs
- *Philippians,* 9 studies by Donald Baker
- *Jonah, Joel and Amos,* 12 studies by Doug and Doris Haugen
- *Christian Character,* 12 studies by Andrea Sterk and Peter Scazzero

Scripture Survey

- *Daniel,* 12 studies by Douglas Connelly
- *New Testament Characters,* 10 studies by Carolyn Nystrom
- *1 & 2 Timothy and Titus,* 11 studies by Pete Sommer
- *Psalms,* 12 studies by Eugene Peterson

Spiritual Formation

- *Christian Disciplines,* 12 studies by Andrea Sterk and Peter Scazzero
- *Prayer,* 12 studies by David Healey
- *God's Love,* 10 studies by Ruth Ann Ridley
- *Praying the Psalms,* 9 studies by Juanita Ryan

Christian Character

- *Christian Character,* 12 studies by Andrea Sterk and Pete Scazzero
- *Integrity,* 10 studies by Carolyn Nystrom

- *Loving Justice,* 12 studies by Bob and Carol Hunter
- *Fruit of the Spirit,* 9 studies by Hazel Offner

Christian Virtues

- *Christian Virtues,* 9 studies by Cindy Bunch
- *Faith,* 9 studies by Dale and Sandy Larsen
- *Hope,* 8 studies by Jack Kuhatschek
- *Love,* 9 studies by Phyllis J. Le Peau
- *Pleasing God,* 9 studies by Jack Kuhatschek

BOOKS ON BIBLE STUDY

Blomberg, Craig L. *The Historical Reliability of the Gospels.* Downers Grove, Ill.: InterVarsity Press, 1987. A strong comprehensive case for the consistency and reliability of Scripture.

Bruce, F. F. *The Canon of Scripture.* Downers Grove, Ill.: InterVarsity Press, 1988. Historical evidence for the acceptance of the canon.

Grahmann, Bob. *Transforming Bible Study.* Downers Grove, Ill.: InterVarsity Press, 2003. An overview of what inductive Bible study is and how to do it from a postmodern perspective.

Guthrie, Donald, ed. *New Bible Dictionary.* 2nd ed. Downers Grove, Ill.: InterVarsity Press, 1991. Comprehensive coverage of books, people, places, terms, doctrines, history, geography, customs and current issues in archaeology and biblical studies.

Keener, Craig. *The IVP Bible Background Commentary: New Testament.* Downers Grove, Ill.: InterVarsity Press, 1993. Useful information on the historical and cultural backgrounds of nearly every verse in the New Testament.

Stuart, Douglas, and Gordon D. Fee. *How to Read the Bible for All Its Worth.* Grand Rapids, Mich.: Zondervan, 1993. The basics of good Bible reading and study.

Wenham, G. J., et al., eds. *New Bible Commentary.* 4th ed. Downers Grove, Ill.: InterVarsity Press, 1994. Solid, concise commentaries on every book of the Bible.

PART FOUR

OUTREACH

This chapter is divided into a number of sections. The first part contains general ideas for gaining a vision for outreach. The next section, "Show to Tell," is focused on serving individuals and the community. The third section deals with reaching seekers with the gospel. The fourth section deals with world mission. The fifth section has ideas for social action. The reading list at the end of the chapter gives resources for each of these areas.

DEVELOPING AN OUTREACH VISION

DREAM ABOUT OUTREACH

After your group has decided how it will reach out to others, use this exercise in planning.

1. Identify the people.

- Who are they?

- Where are they?

- What are their major interests?

- What barriers stand in the way of them hearing the gospel? of their understanding and responding?

- What is their greatest felt need? How could we help meet that need?

2. Pray for the people.

- List ways you can pray for these people.

- Discuss ways you may be used as answers to those prayers.

- Take action accordingly.

3. Get involved.

- What would we like to see happen in the lives of the people we are serving?

- What are some ways to involve ourselves in this?

- What materials do we need for this?

- Do we need further training? What? When? Where?

- What prayer requests for ourselves do we make before God?

PRAY ABOUT OUTREACH

Here are some areas of prayer as your group grows in its vision for outreach.

- For areas of your community and groups that have not been reached with the gospel.

- For opportunities to begin sharing the gospel with friends who do not believe in Jesus Christ as Savior and Lord.

- For short- and long-term missionaries from your church or fellowship.

- For your church or fellowship leadership teams.

- For issues in the newspaper and the countries affected.

- For different parts of the world—one week pray for Eastern Europe, the next week pray for Africa, and so on. *Operation World*, MARC's unreached people prayer guides (919 West Huntington Drive, Monrovia, CA 91016) and 10/40 Window prayer cards (Caleb Project, 10 West Dry Creek Circle, Littleton, CO 80120) are possible resources for prayer requests.

- For people you know around the world—concentrate on Europe, and pray for all those you know involved in ministry there. Next week concentrate on the Middle East, then on Oceania and so on.

SKIT NIGHT
Marsha Petty

Spend one small group session working on a skit to present for a large group or a church meeting to inspire others to get involved in outreach. Or create a skit to reach seekers and perform in a public area. Make the planning session a party and a break from the group's routine. Plan and practice a skit together, then have pizza or donuts. This is a great community builder.

STUDY
In your small group read and discuss books on evangelism, social issues or world missions such as *Good News About Injustice, Out of the Saltshaker, Speaking of Jesus, Get the Word Out* and *Daughters of Hope.*

TRAIN

- Attend a missions or evangelism conference as a small group (such as the Urbana Mission Convention).

- Contact Discover the World (3244 E. Orange Grove Blvd., Pasadena, CA 91107) for church-oriented training programs to mobilize members for missions, or Global Opportunities (1600 Elizabeth St., Pasadena, CA 91104) for tentmaking resources. U.S. Center for World Missions (1605 Elizabeth St., Pasadena, CA 91104) has seminars, books and videos available.

- Focus on the needs of a specific cultural group—especially one in your part of the country. Zwemer Institute (Box 365, Altadena, CA 91001) has resources and seminars on Islam. Overseas Mission Fellowship (10 West Dry Creek Circle, Littleton, CO 80120) offers Chinese Awareness Seminars.

- Recruit from your group those ready for Student Training in Missions or Overseas Training Camp or some other short-term missions experience.

- Use videos to train in evangelism: 2100 Productions' "He Is Not Silent" covers the basic content of the gospel through music, stories, animation and mime; "Stained Images" looks at stereotypes non-Christians have about Christianity; "Out of the Saltshaker," "Give Me an Answer" and "Speaking of Jesus" give training in talking with others about Christ. Also check out the "Contagious Christian" video from Willow Creek Association.

- Tell each other what you have been learning through reading, personal experiences and relationships with others.

SHOW TO TELL: SERVING INDIVIDUALS AND THE COMMUNITY

EMPHASIZE SERVICE
Murphy Belding

There are several reasons to develop a group service project.

- *To apply the Bible to real life.* First John 3:16 says, "This is how we know what love is: Jesus Christ laid down his life for us. And we ought to lay down our lives for our brothers."

- *To work through any group conflict or group fatigue.* Sometimes group conflict happens because members don't feel comfortable relationally. A few hours at a halfway house peeling potatoes together will break down relational barriers.

- *To have fun and laugh together.* Last Christmas one of our groups spent the day at a Salvation Army Christmas-package facility sorting Christmas presents for children. It was a day of laughter and goofiness. This project launched the group into significant discussion at later group meetings.

Here are a few service ideas to get you started:

- Go to a grocery store and help people load their groceries in their car.

- On a rainy night, offer to hold an umbrella for customers as they leave a grocery store and walk to their car.

- Offer to provide child-care at no charge for young families in your church.

- On a hot summer day, pass out free soft drinks to people leaving a local shopping mall. Put one of your church's business cards under the pop-up tab with a handwritten invitation to attend worship.

- Adopt a single college student who isn't from your area and help provide for some of his or her needs while in college.

- Contact a business executive in your community who doesn't attend your church. Ask him if there is something your small group could do for a couple of hours to help him out. He'll think you're crazy, but your group will have fun being together.

GRAFFITI BE GONE
Keith Wright

Throw a graffiti clean-up party. Gather buckets, scrub brushes, sandpaper and hoses. Concentrate on a single area, and you can achieve tangible results in one day.

THE GREAT BANQUET
Sue Sage

After studying the parable of the great banquet, it's fun to prepare your own banquet, which can be as simple as investing in a lot of pizza. Have an open dinner at church or in the dorm, and invite everyone that you see to come and enjoy the feast with you.

MORNING MUFFINS
Sue Sage

Make a couple dozen muffins and a couple containers of juice, and place them in an easily accessible place at your workplace or on your campus for people to enjoy.

PRETTIFY A PARK
Keith Wright

Is there a neglected park in your neighborhood? Get permission from the appropriate local agency, then roll up your sleeves. You'll need trash bags, work gloves, brooms and gardening tools. Bring large pieces of screen to sift broken glass, gum and dangerous objects from sandboxes. You may also need tools for repairing fences. Paint hopscotch and foursquare courts on the asphalt. Ask local businesses to donate fresh sand or tan bark. Expect plenty of onlookers. Perhaps you could invite the curious to a cookout at the park to celebrate its restoration.

SERVE THE COLLEGE CAMPUS
Sue Sage and Allen Lincoln

- Focus your outreach to freshmen during orientation week through setting up book tables (have brochures about your ministry available) at activities fairs, hosting dorm discussions, sponsoring fun events like movies, dances, picnics and volleyball games, helping new students move into dorms and apartments, or doing a door-to-door welcome.

- Distribute care packages during finals or at some other high stress time. You can include fruit, aspirin, cough drops, blue books and #2 pencils, crazy stress-relief toys like those bouncy balls, cookies, granola bars or tea—anything that is conducive to study or stress relief.

- Find a way to do something simple for people as a practical example of God's love for them—no strings attached! By doing this you'll make your church or organization more visible and give a taste of grace. For example, here's a plan for cleaning dorm rooms as a small group:

  1. Make teams of two to cover a floor or series of suites (make sure someone on your team actually lives in the dorm) during a time when students are there.

  2. Choose a bunch of things you can offer (for example, sweeping the floor, making a bed, cleaning windows, cleaning a computer screen [yes, this has been popular!] and anything else you can come up with). Make up a sheet to hand to people explaining who you are, what you're offering and why.

Choose One (FREE!)
___sweep your floor
___clean your computer screen
___make your bed
___wash your windows
This is a practical example of God's love for you.
From _____ [the church or ministry sponsoring your group]

The "Choose One" flyer

3. Gather necessary materials (brooms, dustpans, vacuum cleaner, Windex, paper towels)

4. Greet the students in their rooms saying, "Hi! Choose one!" Let the

student check one and return it to you. If you're talkative, you can explain yourself. If not, just point to the answers on the sheet. The only thing you have to be emphatic about is that you really want to sweep their floors. You may want to leave behind a little note, invitation to a small group or a calling card.

5. Get together when you are done to share your experiences and pray for the people you served. Work at continuing contact with the people you served.

TREAT WITHOUT THE TRICKS
Keith Wright

Instead of collecting treats at Halloween, distribute them. One small group dressed in amusing (but nonscary) costumes and distributed sweets at a children's hospital (check with the hospital first). This group was able to pray with some of the children's parents, providing hope and encouragement.

URBAN GARDEN
Keith Wright

Help urban dwellers turn an abandoned city lot into a garden by providing seeds, tools and muscle. Check with local government whether special permits are required. Then set a time to plant the garden with neighborhood residents. As you tend the garden, relationships will grow along with the plants.

WINDOW WASHERS
Patty Pell

In a busy parking lot, wash car windows for free, and leave a little note saying you are part of a small group and tell where it meets.

WITNESSING TO SEEKERS

BUILD RELATIONSHIPS ON CAMPUS
Sue Sage

• Plan activities to which you can bring friends and so stimulate further interest in the gospel—potluck dinners, dorm discussions, Bible studies, popcorn breaks.

- Organize informal activities that allow you to meet people. For example, play with a footbag in a busy part of campus or in a park. Bat the footbag around a circle, the object being to have everyone kick it once for a "hac." You can't use your hands, and you can't apologize when you mess up. This game is contagious, and people can come and go as they please; for some reason, people are not inhibited to join a "hac" circle full of people that they don't know. The sport is low key enough that you can get to know people while playing.

- Sit in the cafeteria during lunches when many people come and go quickly. Set aside an hour for lunch with the main goal of not only getting some food but also of sitting with as many people that you don't know as possible.

CHRISTIANEZE SELF-HELP
Nairy Ohanian

This is a revealing activity that helps in communicating the gospel. Bring stacks of three-by-five index cards (preferably white). Have the group brainstorm all their favorite Christian lingo, spiritual buzzwords and overused church words. Examples that will arise: *salvation, grace, sanctified, holy.* Also include words such as *fellowship, church, Scriptures, worship* and *share.*

Write the words on the blank side of the index cards. Now have group members write alternative words, which define these terms, on the lined side of the card. The goal is to learn and use words that share truth in a simple, relevant way for our nonspiritual friends. For example, for *grace* you might have "Gift, freebie, money can't buy, undeserved good thing." Or for *fellowship:* "Gathering of people, celebration, meeting with Christians."

Have each member make their own packet of cards. Then quiz one another. Encourage everyone to carry their cards with them, learn alternative words and to practice sharing the gospel without Christianeze!

CIRCLE OF DISCIPLES
Tracy K. Altizer

Have the members of the group form a circle. Without giving any clues as to what kind of circle it's supposed to be, have them rearrange repeatedly until they form one with each person facing out, their backs to the inside of the circle. At that point, remind the members that while it may be most comfortable to associate with those within the circle of Christian friends, Jesus calls us to reach out and to go make disciples of others. This is an especially good exercise for closing a retreat.

CIRCLES OF BELONGING
Rick Richardson

It will be helpful for you as a group to challenge each other to get comfortable with a gospel outline that makes sense to you. Rick Richardson describes a unique approach to presenting the gospel in his book *Evangelism Outside the Box*. He has also created a booklet called *Circles of Belonging* that can be given to seekers that presents the gospel. Here it is in brief:

- Begin by asking your friend, "Can I share a picture of God's love for us?" Divide a napkin (or whatever you're drawing on) into four quadrants. Draw a circle with the word *God* in the center. Share the idea that God made the world and each of us in love, to be in relationship with him. You may want to ask why your friend thinks people so seldom feel really connected to God (Genesis 1:1; Deuteronomy 6:5; Mark 12:29-31).

- Add circles to the second quadrant, labeling them as the things we try to replace God with. Share some of the things you have replaced God with in your own life. Ask your friend if they can identify with what you're describing (Romans 3:23; Ephesians 2:1-2).

- When you talk about the lack of God in the center, write the word *death* over the second quadrant.

- Draw a circle in the third quadrant. Write the name Jesus just above the center of the circle. Draw four arrows pointing to Jesus' name (in the shape of a cross) to indicate that Jesus showed people a rightly centered human life (Mark 15:34; John 3:16; Romans 5:8).

- Draw a cross around Jesus' name. Talk about Jesus' death and resurrection, acts of love so that he could live at our center and restore us into a right relationship with God.

- Draw a new circle in the fourth quadrant. Write Jesus' name in the center. Emphasize that Jesus fills the center. Draw arrows pointing out of the center of the circle to indicate how Jesus restores our right relationship with other things in our life.

- Explain that a commitment to Jesus can change your whole life. This may be a good point to share your commitment story. Ask where God is in the person's life. Ask if he or she would like to know how God could be at the center. Add the words *admit, accept* and *ask* to quadrants two, three and four respectively; and explain their meaning. Offer to lead a simple prayer to invite God into the center of your friend's life (John 1:12-13; Romans 6:23; 12:9; 1 Timothy 1:16).

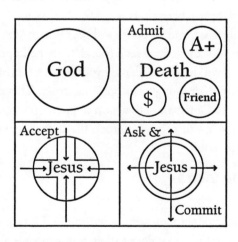

A completed *Circles of Belonging* diagram

Another example of a gospel outline is "First Steps to God." You'll find it on page 137.

COFFEE TALKS
Nina Thiel

Small group members go around their dorm with video cameras and interview their hallmates on camera asking, "When you hear the name Jesus, what do you think?" and "How would you describe your spiritual life?"

A week or so later, the video (having been edited) is shown at a coffeehouse set up in the dorm lounge. The group gets card tables, tablecloths, mugs and good coffee. Small groups from off campus bake and bring really nice desserts and serve the people. Small group members all sit at different tables, and after the video is shown, they initiate conversations about the spiritual issues that came up in the video.

DON'T FORGET TO SHARE YOUR FAITH!
Mike Ortiz and Dale Brady

Here's an idea for those who want to speak to others about Christ but don't know where (or how) to start. Each member ties a string around a finger where it could be easily seen, making a commitment to leave it on for twenty-four hours. Inevitably, others will ask what it's for. You can decide prior to the activity what your response will be. Perhaps "to be thankful for all God has given you" or "to pray for a friend." But the hope is also to start a conversation that will help you identify yourself as a Christian and possibly ask others about their thoughts on spiritual issues. This is a simple way to be identified with Christ and allow him to open up some exciting conversations. When you return to your group the following week, there will be plenty of stories to tell.

DOOR-TO-DOOR VISITS
Brian Parks

Spend a small group meeting reaching out to the dorm or neighborhood where you meet. Pair up and go door to door telling people about the group and inviting them to come sometime. If there's openness, the gospel can be shared. Another idea is to go door to door just asking for prayer requests. The pairs explain that they are Christians and that part of being a Christian is praying for the people around them. Praying for them on the spot is ideal, or leaving, praying and following up later works too.

EMPTY CHAIR
Lyman Coleman

Set up an extra chair for each group meeting and pray for God to fill that chair with a new person. This will help the group keep an attitude of openness to visitors and give members the freedom to invite non-Christian friends.

EVANGELISM TIMELINE
Kelle Ashton

Here's a plan for making evangelism a part of your campus or church group for a year. This will help you to build a vision for outreach into the group from the start, rather than trying to add it in later.

Now and Summer

- Pray for Christians who will be in your group to have an evangelistic attitude.

- Pray for non-Christians to be involved in your group.

September

- Keep praying.

- Meet as many people as possible. Fall is a key time to make connections with new students on campus and a time when churches have many new visitors.

- Invite people to your small group.

- If you are assigned members by a small group coordinator, meet with them individually. Early in the relationship you'll probably get a sense of whether they're Christians or not. Be open and honest, and usually they will too.

- Encourage group members to bring friends.

- Introduce the 2 PLUS plan (see p. 151) and begin praying for non-Christian friends during small group prayer times.

October and November

- If your church or fellowship offers a retreat or evangelism training session, encourage your whole group to attend together.

- Organize a fun, non-threatening activity for your group to do as a whole and to invite your 2 PLUS people to.

December and January

- Support one another in inviting your 2 PLUS people to church or a fellowship meeting or a winter retreat.

February

- If available, as a group activity, go to a training seminar for leading a GIG (Groups Investigating God) on campus or a seeker Bible discussion. Becky Pippert offers seminars through her Salt Shaker Resources ministry. You'll find a schedule at <www.saltshaker.org>. You may want to read her small book *How to Lead a Seeker Bible Discussion*. There are also some tips for leading an investigative group on page 144.

- Challenge one another to ask 2 PLUS people to be in a seeker Bible discussion. You may want to actually have these new people join your group and use appropriate material, or hold a short-term group at another time.

March

- Keep praying for 2 PLUS people and the seeker Bible discussion.

- Consider doing an outreach project as a group during spring vacation. For example, you could join a beach evangelism project or work with Habitat for Humanity.

April

- Encourage one another to explain to the 2 PLUS people who are ready what it means to commit their lives to Christ.

EVANGELISTIC PARTIES

In a fun, relaxed, relational and informal setting, seekers feel freer to express their thoughts and feelings about the claims of Christ. Here are some guidelines for throwing a great evangelistic party:

1. Develop a strategy of using parties to reach out. In your small group look at Scripture for principles on hospitality and relationships. Discuss the party scene in your community or on your campus. Talk about what makes a good party.

2. Decide what you want to do. Capitalize on creativity. Talk about why you want to throw a party and who it's for.

3. Plan the party. Consider where it will take place, how much it will cost, what kind of theme and decorations you'll have, how you'll get the word out, what kind of food you'll have, what kinds of activities you'll have and how both introverts and extroverts will be made comfortable, and who will clean up.

4. Pray for the party.

5. Have the party. Remember to watch the noise, end at a reasonable hour and to have fun.

6. Evaluate the party.

FIRST STEPS TO GOD

InterVarsity Christian Fellowship

The following is an outline of the Christian message that was developed by InterVarsity Christian Fellowship. It is a useful summary to keep in mind as you share your faith. You may want to keep a copy inside your Bible. You can help each other learn it as a small group. Challenge each other to learn a line or a section each week and report in during small group.

God

1. God loves you (John 3:16).

2. God is holy and just. He punishes all evil and expels it from his presence (Romans 1:18).

Humanity

1. God, who created everything, made us for himself to find our purpose in fellowship with him (Colossians 1:16).

2. We rebelled and turned away from God (Isaiah 53:6). The result is separation from God (Isaiah 59:2). The penalty is eternal death (Romans 6:23).

Christ

1. God became a man in the person of Jesus Christ to restore the broken fellowship (Colossians 1:19-20). Christ lived a perfect life (1 Peter 2:22).

2. Christ died as a substitute for us by paying the death penalty for our rebellion (Romans 5:8). He arose (1 Corinthians 15:3-4) and is alive today to give us a new life of fellowship with God, now and forever (John 10:10).

Response

1. I must repent for my rebellion (Matthew 4:17).

2. I must believe Christ died to provide forgiveness and a new life of fellowship with God (John 1:12).

3. I must receive Christ as my Savior and Lord with the intent to obey him. I do this in prayer by inviting him into my life (Revelation 3:20).

Cost

1. Cost to God (1 Peter 1:18-19).

2. No cost to you: your salvation (Ephesians 2:8-9).

3. Cost to you: discipleship (Luke 9:23-24).

FOLLOW UP—A ROLE-PLAY

Ann Beyerlein

You may be unsure about where some group members are with Jesus. What they say in small group gives some idea, but sometimes it is important to follow up their comments and talk to them one-to-one about what they are thinking about spiritual issues. Sometimes the conversation will surprise the leader and can help solidify something in the mind of the member. This can move the member a step closer to becoming a Christian or spur the member on toward spiritual growth.

The leader might just stop by and see a member or ask a member to get together to talk about small group and how things are going spiritually. The leader needs to be ready with a few questions. Beginning with a general question about small group or a question that follows up a comment at small group can be a great way to start. If the person is open, ask about their religious background, what has been significant for them in small group, what they think a Christian is, whether they consider themselves a Christian or what the barriers to their becoming a Christian are. Ask about their spiritual questions or needs. If the person is obviously a Christian, ask about their spiritual growing edge and what they need to go deeper.

The following role-plays for small group leaders will give practice in asking spiritual questions. They can also be used in a small group of Christians to help people practice talking to others about their faith.

The small group members listed are all at different places spiritually. The leader has noticed that all are holding back some in small group. They may not pray or fully participate. All of these people seem a bit stuck spiritually. The leader prays and decides to have a one-to-one conversation to lovingly ask some questions and see if he or she can help these members become unstuck. The person playing the leader should not know the exact situation of the group member beforehand. The fun is in the discovery.

1. Susie won't pray because she's not sure she is a Christian. She has a lot of doubts about what Christianity is about. She feels some guilt about where she is spiritually.

2. John won't pray because he knows he's not a Christian. He's bothered by the suffering in the world. He has no idea why Jesus died on the cross. He thinks there may be a connection between Jesus' death on the cross and how God feels about suffering.

3. Drake has been coming to small group all year. He'd become a Christian if someone would just ask him and explain to him how to receive Christ.

4. Debbie comes to small group about half of the time. The other half of the time she's having too much fun to show up. She's not sure if she is a Christian. She doesn't feel good about her lifestyle, but she doesn't want to give up some of the things she enjoys.

GIVE A TESTIMONY
Ted McMullen

Ask someone in your small group to give a testimony for an investigative study or to encourage other small group members. Choose someone who, first of all, is growing and bearing fruit in his or her life. Second, select someone who can stay in the time frame of three to four minutes and can connect with the theme of the Bible study. Let the person know why he or she was chosen. After the testimony is outlined, have the person run through it so that you can make sure it's on track and within the time frame. Help them to avoid "Christianeze." Don't forget to be encouraging.

Here's an outline for a testimony that shows how faith and good works relate: "I decided to trust Christ as Lord of my life when I was [add specifics]. It has been a process of learning how to obey God and serve others [add examples]. I have prioritized faith, but what I do shows that I have made a decision for Christ and belong to him."

Another approach would be for you to interview another Christian during the meeting. You will need to practice together in advance to make sure you keep within the given timeframe. Here are some interview questions on the topic of lordship:

1. Tell us a little about your life before you understood what it meant to be a Christian.

2. What were some of your ways of acting and dealing with things, and where did they lead you?

3. When did you begin to understand about having a relationship with Christ?

4. What were some things that held you back from giving Christ control or "lordship" of your life?

5. When did you decide to give control of your life to Christ, and what made you willing to do this?

6. What have you noticed to be different about God now compared to what made you hesitant about him before?

7. How would you summarize the changes that have happened in your life since you gave Christ control?

GUIDELINES FOR EVANGELISTIC TALKS
Doug Whallon

An evangelistic talk is a meeting convened in a dormitory or hall of residence (sorority, fraternity or club) or some other public place where the claims of Jesus Christ are presented in a short address or testimony. The intent of the talk may be either evangelistic (containing a direct presentation of the gospel of our Lord Jesus Christ) or pre-evangelistic (focusing on Jesus Christ with the intent of stimulating the listeners to investigate Christ more thoroughly or assessing their personal bankruptcy without Christ). The purpose of such talks is twofold: (1) to provide witness to Jesus Christ and (2) to assist the Christians who live in the residence or community to share Christ by providing a springboard for further conversation.

Suggested Format

1. A word of welcome by a Christian who lives on the floor and a brief but compelling introduction of the speaker.

2. A fifteen-minute presentation or testimony by the speaker that witnesses to Jesus Christ.

3. A fifteen-minute question/answer period (expect anything).

4. A word of thanks by the initial person, explaining the booklets that are freely available and how they may be obtained (circulate a sign-up list to receive booklets).

5. Prompt dismissal, although further interaction is welcomed.

Who Should Come?

- Non-Christians living in your dorm or community.

- Christians who bring with them one or more of their friends who are non-Christians.

- Young Christians who will grow in faith and confidence as a result.

Topic Selection

- Be stabbing and thought-provoking.

- Focus on personal needs and problems.

- Be self-explanatory.

- Accurately describe the content (do not be deceptive).

Example Topics from Larry Thiel

- Would a Good God Send a Good Person to Hell?

- Sex, Drugs, and Rock and Roll: Is God Part of the Good Life?

- Christianity on Trial

- Evidence for the Christian Faith

- If God Is so Loving, Why Is the World so Messed Up?

- Death, the Final Frontier (Is There Life After Death?)

- Would Jesus Attend a Frat Party?

The Role of the Sponsoring Small Group

1. Pray as a small group before, during and after the event. Inform others who will pray.

2. Determine a leader who can coordinate the mechanics and help delegate different responsibilities.

3. Gain permission from appropriate authorities to use the lounge or meeting room (usually the RA has this responsibility).

4. Contact and confirm your speaker, specifying when, where, what, how long and why.

5. Publicize.

- One week in advance put up posters describing basic information.

- During the last week, invite friends.

- Fifteen minutes in advance, remind people by knocking on doors of people on the floor (avoid being obnoxious).

6. Food (soda, juice, popcorn, chips, cookies) encourages people to hang out afterward and ask questions or talk in small clusters.

7. Room organization do's and don'ts (from Larry Thiel):

- Do have the speaker away from the entrance to the lounge so people will feel comfortable trickling in and out.

- Don't put the refreshments by the door—the goal is to get people to stick around and get into conversations.

- Don't have small group members sit together. Do have small group members spread out and sit among the friends they bring.

- Don't have group members talk to the speaker after the talk. Do have them talk with the people around them about the talk and the gospel.

8. The day after the talk, have Christians bring the specified booklets to those who indicated a desire for literature; this is a great opportunity to inquire about their reaction and to converse about Christ.

9. Write a thank-you note to the speaker.

IF JESUS IS THE ANSWER, WHAT ARE THE QUESTIONS?

This self-assessment will help you to be aware of people's needs so you can better communicate the gospel.

1. Take time to think about your own life. What are the major questions that you face in life? Write them down.

2. Think about one or more of your non-Christian friends. What are their major questions about life?

3. Compare your list with those of your friends. Most people doing this exercise find that their own questions are not that different from those of their friends.

4. How has the message of the gospel given you answers to your questions? Think through each question and write down how the gospel is "good news" to you. Think about the questions of your friends. How is the gospel good news to them? How would you communicate this good news in a way that they would understand it?

INTEREST SURVEY
Peter Cha

The sample survey on page 145 can be used to find out what topics seekers are interested in. Use this with a group of people you'd like to reach. You could use it in a workplace or neighborhood. Or, on a college campus you could survey a dorm or a fraternity group on potential dorm talk topics they might like to hear. This can also be a great conversation starter.

LEADING AN INVESTIGATIVE BIBLE STUDY
Ada Lum (Adapted from How to Begin an Evangelistic Bible Study *by Ada Lum [Downers Grove, Ill.: InterVarsity Press, 1971].)*

1. Use a modern translation of the Bible, because it is easier to follow when everyone has the same wording. If you have the same edition, then you can just give the page number. (When not everyone is familiar with the Bible, it is less embarrassing than fumbling around trying to find 1 John.) Make sure you have extra Bibles on hand.

2. Prepare with a co-leader. It really helps. Pray together too!

3. Set some ground rules for discussion, and explain them at the first meeting and whenever a new member joins the group.

4. Be enthusiastic. Relax.

5. Don't be uptight about setting doctrine straight as questions or comments raise concerns.

6. Be excited that they are discovering something from the Bible, even if

it's not quite accurate yet.

7. Avoid answering your own questions. Be comfortable with silences. Remember, they haven't spent the time you have in finding answers to these questions, so they are probably busy looking and thinking.

8. Pray regularly for your friends that God will open their spiritual understanding and kindle in them an interest and a longing to know him.

Which questions interest you most? Number your top three.

___ Why do you say that Jesus Christ is the only way to God?

___ Aren't there many ways to God?

___ Isn't it enough to live a good life?

___ Does it matter what you believe as long as you are sincere?

___ How could a loving God send people to hell?

___ Why do innocent people suffer?

___ Isn't believing in Jesus irrational?

___ Isn't the New Testament full of errors?

___ Why do Christians think they know how other people should live?

___ I'm happy. Why do I need Jesus?

___ _____(fill in your own question)

yes no (circle one) Would you be interested in a workshop or discussion group on one of your top three questions?

If yes, leave your name and phone number, and we'll contact you.

Name _____

Phone _____

---

9. Love group members as friends, real people, not "souls to be saved." Let them enrich your life, learn from them and affirm them.

10. Follow through after the study (when it seems appropriate) with some questions that let them know you are interested in them and have been thinking about what they have said or are grappling with. For example, "What have you been learning from the study?" "Have your ideas about God changed since you've been studying the Bible?"

Remember, we dare not pressure people. God doesn't barge his way in, so we must follow his example and be sensitive in our inquiries.

PUBLIC TALKS AND DEBATES
Brian Hossink

- Depending on your context, these talks can be as general and nonthreatening as a topic like "What's Wrong with the World Today" to something as confrontational as "How a Loving God Can Send People to Hell." You can focus the talk in one dorm or open it in a public area.

- Set up a debate between a Christian professor or staffworker and an atheist professor. Planning and care is required to make sure this is run properly, but it can reap many rewards as people see that Christians can and do use their intellect.

STUDY QUESTIONS
These questions can help to bring out the uniqueness and the authority of Jesus as the God-man.

- In what specific ways does Jesus show his interest in people as individuals? his understanding of their basic human needs and not just outward ones? What does he see in people and their human dilemmas that others apparently do not see? In what ways do his attitudes to people and their predicaments contrast with those of his contemporaries?

- What do you learn about human nature from Jesus' viewpoint? What does he command? What does he condemn?

- What happens when Jesus takes on the problems of his society: corruption, pride, ignorance, evil, cruelty, sickness, materialism? What traditions and prejudices does he come up against in doing so?

- How does Jesus affect people? Why? How do they affect him? Why? How does he bring out the best in people? How does he affirm their personal worth?

- What "human interest" details do you observe? What unique aspects of Jesus' personality and character does this event reveal? What fresh insights into his life and mission do you now have?

- What are the implications of Jesus' life and Word for us today? What practical thing can you do this week to employ the truth you have learned?

These questions are only broad guidelines for your personal study. They need specific rewording for your particular group. For example, if you are studying John 3:1-15, which records Jesus' conversation with the religious aristocrat Nicodemus, you will not want to ask, "How does Jesus show his interest in individuals?" Instead, use a sequence of questions that will precipitate insights: "What did Jesus already know about Nicodemus?" "Look at Jesus' response to Nicodemus's opening statement in verse 2. What hidden question did Jesus apparently see behind it?" "If Jesus could understand Nicodemus so well, what do you think he understands about people today—you, for example?"

TAKE YOUR SMALL GROUP TO THE PEOPLE
Dan Lentz

People are most effectively reached when you go to them rather than expecting them to come to you—to visit your church or small group, for example. Further, small groups that have the dual function of nurturing Christians and reaching seekers often face internal conflict about their goals. One solution to these tensions is the "O-group Strategy."

Imagine the members of your group arranged in a circle of intimate nurturing relationships with one another. Most of our traditional thought processes about group outreach center on how to bring more new people into the circle. This creates conflict about what the small group should be—is it for seekers or Christians?

What if instead of trying to bring a new person to the next group meeting, we set a goal of faithfully investing our life in Christ in one or two others outside the group—where they are most effectively reached? Then after you have begun to develop those relationships and established trust, you might make a suggestion that you read a book together that offers a biblical perspective on some interest you share. A group member might reach out to one or two or more people. Now a small group member has established a whole new group: an O (outreach)-group.

This O-group is not isolated from the main group because while these O-group relationships are being established, the original small group is praying for these O-group individuals by name. Group members are also sharing with their O-group friends about what a great experience the regular small group is to them and even inviting their O-group person to share a meal with another small group member occasionally. Pretty soon, every small group member has people they are reaching out to and your small group picture starts to look something like the figure below.

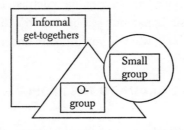

Small groups reaching out through O-groups

O-group people move easily into the small group circle because over time other people from the group have also entered into a relationship with them. When the day comes for the O-group person to come to a regular group meeting, it's almost like they are regulars. But the goal is not to ask people to come to our small group—we are trying to take the small group to them so that we can make an ongoing relationship-based connection to someone who needs Christ.

TALK ABOUT IT
Kelle Ashton

Have each person share their fears about evangelism or any bad experiences with evangelism. Talk about the fears and determine one step each person needs to take to overcome their fears. Then commit to pray for each other's accomplishing their next step and overcoming their fears.

THIRTY-DAY EVANGELISM PLAN
Len Andyshak (Taken from Thirty-Day Evangelism Plan *by Len Andyshak [Downers Grove, Ill.: InterVarsity Press, 1986].)*

Those of us who have become Jesus' disciples realize that we are to be becoming fishers of humanity and to be going to all the world. However, we often feel our attempts at fishing to be very inadequate, or we simply do no fishing at all. It has been well said that one learns to fish only by fishing. This experience is designed to help you get started. It is simple enough to be done by anyone, practical enough to actually produce some changes and stretching enough to keep you depending on the Lord and reminded that this whole process is absolutely miraculous and not contingent on your limited abilities and strength. You can follow this plan as a small group, offering each other encouragement and accountability along the way. Each week you can talk and pray about what you are learning.

To say it simply, seven things are involved over thirty days. (If you would feel more biblical and assured we could make it seven things and forty days.) One small group member can create a chart of all the activities for each member of the group to use, checking them off each day.

Daily Prayer

Start each day with a simple, specific prayer—something like this: "Here I am, Lord; please heal me, strengthen me, introduce me to the people you want me to love, and please give me opportunities to share with them about you. Amen."

Daily Reading

During the thirty days you read a book—about five pages a day. (Done daily, it provides continued input and encouragement and never becomes a burden.) Two good options are *Get the Word Out* by John Teter and *Out of the Saltshaker* by Rebecca Manley Pippert.

Meeting People

Over the thirty days introduce yourself to fifteen to twenty new people. This can be done anywhere or in any way the Lord leads in answer to the prayer you prayed. Perhaps sitting by someone in class, saying hello and getting their name. Perhaps at a meal, in the shower, running, in the store. Who knows what the Lord may do! Record the names of the people you meet on your chart, and review them daily so you don't forget them (a deadly sin in evangelism).

Casual Time

Four times during the month (once a week) spend some time with a non-Christian friend or acquaintance. It could be the same person each time or four different people. Possibly it will be one of the fifteen to twenty new people you have met. This should be a casual, nonreligious activity of some kind—have a latte, go to a funny movie, study together, go to a party or go roller-blading. Record what you did on your chart.

Invitations

Four other times (once a week again) invite one of your non-Christian friends to a "religious" activity. They don't have to accept—you just have to invite them! The invitation could be to church, a Bible study or an evangelistic talk. You could even be daring and invite them to look at Jesus in the Bible with you for a few weeks (but beware of this type of boldness; you never know what might happen—to you or them!).

Ask About Jesus

Twice you will simply ask a person what they think about Jesus. You might start by first asking about their church background and if they are still involved. Then move to the question of Jesus. It will get you to the heart of the matter quickly and easily. You will find people surprisingly open with you, especially after having established even a brief friendship with you before this point. As always the key is to be sensitive to the Lord's guidance—the right person (perhaps not the one you expected), at the right time (perhaps at an inconvenient time or when you are sure you're not ready yet). Remember that simple prayer—he will hear, and he will answer. You can expect some miraculous opportunities and the wisdom from above in that moment. "'Not by might nor by power, but by my Spirit,' says the LORD" (Zechariah 4:6).

Unlimited Possibilities

At the end of the thirty days, choose one to three specific goals to continue your evangelistic momentum in the immediate future. The possibilities include 2 PLUS Evangelism, a one-to-one evangelistic Bible discussion or joining a club to meet non-Christians. Each small group member should do this, and the group can continue to encourage each other to follow through on their commitments.

2 PLUS EVANGELISM

The commitment of 2 PLUS evangelism is to pray consistently for the conversion of two friends and for boldness in taking opportunity to witness to them.

Steps to Live Out 2 PLUS

- Acknowledge dependence on God's grace to draw your friends to Christ.
- Identify two not-yet Christians for whom you will pray.
- Develop a friendship with them.
- Choose a prayer partner, and pray together for your friends.

While I Pray, I Build My Friendship Through . . .

- Spending weekly time with them
- Learning more about them: sports, hobbies, major, arts, experience with other Christians, beliefs about Christ
- Looking for ways to serve them

- Taking risks by inviting them to Bible study, chapter meeting, read a Christian book, church, social events

- Sharing the gospel with them

  I will pray for (list names):

  1. _____

  2. _____

  My prayer partner is_____.

  My next step(s) to live out 2 PLUS are_____.

USE FILM, VIDEO AND TV IN EVANGELISM

Alan MacDonald

The media can provide an excellent catalyst for discussion in a variety of settings. Here is a partial list of videos that are good discussion starters. Use the whole film or just a segment, allowing time afterward for discussion. Preview any video you intend to use (don't just rely on your memory). This will help you to formulate discussion questions and allow you to anticipate any scenes that are inappropriate for your intended audience. What may seem like innocent sex scenes to some may be too arousing for others.

Films You May Want to Use

Babbette's Feast (G)—Story of a Parisian refugee who goes to live with two spinster daughters of a minister in a small Danish village. Themes of servanthood, joy and celebration. (1987, Danish)

Broadcast News (R)—Focuses on the TV news world and the relationship between three characters. Brings up a variety of issues, including ethics and friendship. (1987)

Chariots of Fire (PG)—Story of two men who run in the 1924 Olympics. Contains themes relating to the tension between Christian and secular values and motivations. (1981)

Crimes and Misdemeanors (PG-13)—A Woody Allen film that weaves two different but related stories together. Themes of betrayal, trust, morality, guilt. (1989)

Cry Freedom (PG)—Story about South African activist's friendship with a newspaper editor. Themes of racism, social justice. (1987)

Dead Poets Society (PG)—Story of an English teacher and his prep school students. Themes include purpose and motivation in life, individualism versus conformity and authority issues. (1989)

Driving Miss Daisy (PG)—Relationship between a cantankerous older woman and her chauffeur. Themes of loyalty, friendship, racism, old age. (1989)

Field of Dreams (PG-13)—Story of a farmer who ends up building a baseball diamond on his property. Themes of faith, reconciliation, hope, family. (1989)

Fried Green Tomatoes (PG-13)—Two stories—one of life in a small southern town and the other of a relationship between two women. Themes of friendship and aging, among others. (1991)

Grand Canyon (R)—Focuses on several interrelated lives, the issues each is facing and how they each respond to traumatic events in their lives. (1991)

Jesus of Montreal (R)—A group of actors come together for a production of the Passion play. Themes of religious hypocrisy and commercialism, among others. (1989, French Canadian)

The Mission (PG)—Follows Jesuit mission in Brazilian jungle. Issues relating to crosscultural missions, true faith, justice. (1986)

Mosquito Coast (PG)—Idealistic inventor moves his family to a remote South American village where he attempts to play God. Issues of crossing cultures, control, family. (1986)

Places in the Heart (PG)—A widow determined to survive as a farmer takes in boarders. Deals with racism, poverty, death. (1984)

Say Anything (PG-13)—A loner in high school goes after the class brain and is surprised by what he finds. Themes of friendship, betrayal, self image. (1989)

Stand by Me (R)—Boyhood friendship between four boys. Themes of friendship, community. (1986)

The Trip to Bountiful (PG)—Story of an elderly woman who longs to see her childhood home. Themes of Christian faith, valuing people. (1985)

Tucker (PG)—True story of an entrepreneurial carmaker in the forties who is squeezed out by other carmakers. Issues of integrity, success/failure, business ethics. (1988)

Wall Street (R)—Young hotshot enters the world of Wall Street. Themes of greed, compromise, ethics, family loyalty. (1987)

Here are some questions you can use to discern the underlying values of a TV show or film.

- What is the premise of the movie? Does it agree or conflict with biblical truth?

- Who are the heroes? Who are the villains? Who are the Christians and/ or religious characters in the film?

- How is the world portrayed? the government? evil?

- How is reality portrayed? What are the worldviews of the characters?

- How is love portrayed? the family?

- Would you be embarrassed (or offended) to sit through the movie with your parents or Jesus?

- What are the redemptive elements in the film, and are they enough to offset the destructive elements?

For more information see *Movies in Close Up* by Alan MacDonald (Downers Grove, Ill.: InterVarsity Press, 1992).

WORKPLACE SURVEY
Rob Stroud

Ask a few colleagues at work to jot down in five lines or less what they think is the meaning of life. If they ask, tell them that you will use their thoughts in your church's small group as you are discussing this matter. This exercise helped my small group better understand people's questions and prepare how to answer them. In addition, I had a prolonged and friendly discussion with three work colleagues over lunch.

WORLD MISSION

BOOKS FOR THE WORLD

Collect used Christian books, videos, Bibles and magazines from chapter members and send them overseas for students in English-speaking IFES movements who have few resources of their own. To find out what countries have requested books, contact IFES World Headquarters, 55 Palmerston Road, Harrow, Middlesex HA3 7RR, England.

GIVE

Offer financial support to

- a church friend who is working as a missionary

- people going on short-term missions projects

- an IFES staffworker or IFES twinning partner (contact IFES—IV-Link, P.O. Box 7895, Madison, WI 53707)

- an IVCF staffworker (minority staff and Black campus ministers are especially in need of support)

- the outreach ministry of your church

LEAD AN INTERNATIONAL STUDY
Tom Sirinides

Your group is likely to have a wonderfully diverse mix of people from many different backgrounds. These guidelines were created for leaders of the Rutgers International Christian Fellowship to help them understand the unique needs of the group:

1. Gear the language and pace of the discussion to those who are unfamiliar with the Bible, with English, or with both. Avoid the use of Christian terms and jargon whenever possible. If others in the group

use them, pause to make a general explanation of the term.

2. After the passage has been read, ask if there are any questions about words, and offer definitions as necessary.

3. Watch for a confused or puzzled look on the face of a group member. Ask them if they have a question. They may be totally lost, or only slightly confused, but in either case the anxiety of the situation can make it hard to think—especially in a foreign language (which English is to many in our group).

4. Try to be aware as well of when a quieter member seems to be thinking, or starts to speak but is unwittingly cut off by a more vocal member of the group. People are often struggling to formulate their thoughts (again, an especially difficult thing to do in a foreign language), and unless someone such as you, the leader, pauses the flow of the discussion on their behalf, their thoughts may not come together fully until after the conversation has already moved on. Just saying, "Bill, did you want to say something?" can be enough to facilitate this process.

5. Some application questions are not suitable for a group such as ours, with many non-Christians. In preparing and leading, it is helpful to seek an application that is of relevance to both Christians and non-Christians alike. Use this as the study's conclusion. Christians and non-Christians have many common concerns (strength to deal with hardship, peace in the midst of stress and pressure, hope for the future), so an application of this type will be meaningful to a broader audience than one about altering your prayer life or witnessing more fervently, for example. These things are important, but not always suitable for our group. Our goal is that everyone would see the relevance of the Bible to their own life today, whether they are Christians yet or not.

6. Also regarding application questions: Using the approach of "Here's something to think about" can work well in a group with non-Christians, and especially with many East Asians. ("Saving face" is very important in most cultures of East Asia.) People can feel threatened by a request to verbally discuss their failings and sins in a group set-

ting. But a "thought question" causes people to consider the relevance of the passage to their lives without forcing them to disclose it publicly. Rather than putting the pressure on members to "open up" (which can distract people from the question and focus them on their fears), a thought question both frees them to respond to the study and leaves the door open for meaningful one-to-one conversations afterward.

7. Remember: You as the leader are the "guardian" of the discussion. Try to see that there is fairly balanced participation in the study. Don't let a few members (usually those who are quite familiar with English or with the Bible) dominate things or move the discussion along too quickly. Don't let other group members (often those who are fairly new to English or to the Bible) feel left out. Encourage the more talkative members to hold back, and seek to draw out the quieter ones.

8. Depending on the international student(s), they may or may not feel comfortable with verbal prayer. (Some appreciate being prayed for regardless.) One student from Taiwan found that the prayer time forced her to deal with the battle she was feeling. "Pray for me because Buddha doesn't want me to believe this," she said. She later became a Christian. (Jane Pelz)

9. Above all, ask God for wisdom and guidance as you lead. He has promised to provide it for us if we ask him.

REACH OUT TO INTERNATIONALS

People who are new to a country will greatly appreciate your friendship and help in making the transition and understanding the culture. Any university campus is likely to have international students, and many metropolitan areas will also have people who are new to the countries. Refugee placement centers may be able to give you names of international people with particular needs. (Contact World Relief, 7 East Baltimore St., Baltimore, MD 21202, 443/451-1900 as well as university admissions centers.)

- To develop vision for reaching international people, study Genesis together. This will help you better understand the Abrahamic covenant and God's plan for the whole world of using the Jews to call the Gentiles to himself. (Jane Pelz)

- Help internationals adjust to our culture and experience your city: meet them at the airport, help them move into dorms or apartments, show them around the university, show them around the city, hold socials to which you can invite them, invite them home for weekends or holidays.

- Plan special events such as a joint InterVarsity/International Student Club get-together. (Jane Pelz)

- Pray weekly for international friends.

- Invite Christian international students to join your small group. (Jane Pelz)

- Attend the international club or another ethnic club. (Jane Pelz)

- Plan a worship service with a church of a different ethnic group. You will learn from one another's worship traditions and strengths. Many members may be recent immigrants or people who are still learning English. Keep in mind, however, that there may also be a second or third generation of people in the church who were born in the United States and are completely acclimated to the culture.

- Lead an international Bible study geared toward non-Christians or people who are still learning English. Begin by inviting some friends or acquaintances over, and ask them if they would be interested in studying the Bible together. Meet in a reserved room in the library, an empty classroom or a dorm room. (Jane Pelz)

- Watch cartoons together. Cartoons have simplified language for those who are still learning, and cartoons about the Bible are a launching point for Bible study. The Family Entertainment Network cartoons deal with the stories of the Old Testament and some of the gospel stories. The cartoons bring Jesus and his teachings to life, and it is much easier for the group to discuss the passage. The Superbook Cartoon about Adam and Eve can be used to study the first three chapters in Genesis. This cuts down on the time spent explaining the various English words in the Bible that are not familiar and allows for more time to interact. (Will and Vittoria Grant)

- Nairy Ohanian suggests an activity for international students called "Around the World." It allows the students to reconnect with home and share history, and it serves as a springboard for missions prayer! Bring eight-by-fifteen-inch paper (if possible) and colored markers, and have each group member draw a world map as best as they can, or bring photocopies of world maps. On their maps, people locate where they were born, where their family now lives, one country they have visited, one country they want to visit in the future and one country they would like to pray for and why. Share drawings with the group; then pray for the countries indicated for prayer. Pray for families too, if time permits. Encourage group members to take their maps home and use them to continue praying for missions.

READ A MISSIONARY BIOGRAPHY
All group members can read and discuss a book, or one group member can read and report back. William Carey Library (P.O. Box 40129, Pasadena, CA 91114) and STL Books (Box 28, Waynesboro, GA 30830) are good sources of missionary biographies. Write for a catalog.

SHORT-TERM MISSIONS
Some agencies (including IVCF Global Projects and STIM) will take your whole group as a team. Personal and group development from such an experience is tremendous. If it is not possible to go as a whole group, you can send one member of your group. Here are some ways to support that person.

- Pray for the spiritual, physical and emotional preparation of your member. Pray also for the people with whom and to whom she or he will be going.

- Help in fundraising.

- Help address, stuff and mail prayer letters.

- Go shopping for items needed for the trip.

- Do research on the country and people your friend will be serving.

- Make and eat meals together that will be similar to the food your member will be eating.

- Buy gifts that your member can give during the trip.

- Make a journal for the member to read at intervals throughout the short-term. Have each member write an encouraging note and put a date to be read on it.

- Plan a going-away party or packing party.

- See your member off at the airport.

- Assign weeks throughout the short-term for members to write to the short-termer.

- Meet the short-termer at the airport upon return.

- Be patient and provide opportunity for your friend to talk about their time away. Help him or her focus by asking questions.

- Encourage the short-termer to take time to readjust to life here.

- Pray with your friend about people he or she met, the ministry that went on, for continuance in the ministry, for an understanding of next steps.

SPONSOR A MISSIONARY
Brian Hossink

Get the name of a missionary from your denomination or your staffworker. Pray regularly for the missionary, take a donation (or do a fundraiser like collecting soda cans and returning them for cash), read letters from the missionary and pray about specific requests, and send letters weekly to let your missionary know that they are being prayed for. Send birthday cards and care packages of items they need. Send newspaper articles about trends and important events to keep them informed of life back home. If it's available to you and the missionary, e-mail is the best way to keep in touch with people overseas.

SOCIAL ACTION

DEFINE JUSTICE

Jana Webb (Adapted from Economic Justice, *a Global Issues Bible Study [Downers Grove, Ill.: InterVarsity Press, 1990].)*

Read Amos 2:6-7; 4:1-2; 5:11; 6:4-7; 8:4-6; 9:8. From these verses how would you define our call to the ministry of justice? Pray together for hearts of justice. Read Matthew 25:31-46. Who are the hungry, thirsty, strangers, naked and prisoners in your community? How can you minister to their needs?

ENVIRONMENTAL STEWARDSHIP

Ruth Goring (Adapted from Environmental Stewardship, *a Global Issues Bible Study [Downers Grove, Ill.: InterVarsity Press, 1990].)*

Here are a few ideas that will help you to be more aware of God's creation. You can do them as a group or on your own with follow-up discussion.

- Take a hike or stroll through a park. Sit down on the grass or on a rock and contemplate your surroundings—the variegations in a rock, the patterns of tree bark, the veins of a leaf. Think of the pleasure God took in creating these things.

- Take a walk and pick up litter as you go, or find a vacant lot that needs some cleanup and go to it.

- Contact a local biologist or conservation group and find out whether any plant or animal species in your area is endangered because of human activity and what you can do about it.

- Read Genesis 1:1—2:25, and make a list of what the passage teaches regarding the relationship between human beings and the rest of the created order.

- Keep track of your car's mileage and have it checked for polluting emissions. Can you use less gas by taking the bus, riding a bike, carpooling or walking?

- Read aloud Psalm 96 and spend time worshiping God for his generous sustenance of his creatures.

- Buy organically grown food or talk to your grocer about your desire to have organically grown produce.

- Do a bit of gardening. If you don't have a place to plant, find out about renting space (usually very cheap) in a public space. Or if someone in the small group has the land, work on a garden together. If your church has enough land, consider establishing a community garden, inviting others from the church and neighborhoods to come and take a plot.

- Read Hosea 4:1-3 and discuss the relationship between our treatment of one another and our harmony with the land.

- Begin composting vegetable wastes (rinds, pulp, eggshells, seeds). Simply bury your wastes in your gardening area, or deliver them regularly to someone who gardens.

- Talk to a Christian farmer about the issues he or she faces in working the land lovingly.

- Solicitation letters and other junk mailings are often printed on only one side of a sheet of paper. Save these sheets and use them for notes and memos. When both sides have been used, recycle.

- Water—so ordinary, so taken for granted—is a wonderful gift from God. Examine your water-use habits. Perhaps you can take shorter showers. Dishwashers use much more water and electricity than hand washing. A commercial car wash is likewise much more extravagant than bucket-and-rag-style washing. How can you save water?

- Often people from Two-Thirds World countries can help us see what is wasteful about our lifestyle. Talk to an international person about these issues, and find out what ideas he or she has.

- Plan an Earthkeeping Day for your fellowship, campus, church or community. Talk about what God has been unfolding for you about our responsibilities toward the earth, and offer resources to help others begin to practice and earthkeeping ethic.

- Read a book about environmental stewardship, such as *Earthkeeping* edited by Loren Wilkinson (Grand Rapids: Eerdmans, 1980) or *Redeeming Creation* edited by Fred C. Van Dyke (Downers Grove, Ill.: InterVarsity Press, 1996).

- Get involved with organizations that promote environmental concerns, such as Co-Op America (2100 M St., NW, Suite 310, Washington, D.C. 20063, 202/872-5307), Eco-Justice Working Group (475 Riverside Dr., New York, NY 10115, 202/872-5307), Greenpeace (1436 U St. NW, Washington, D.C. 20009, 202/462-1177), National Wildlife Federation (1400 16th St. NW, Washington, D.C. 20036, 202/797-6800) or Sierra Club (730 Polk St., San Francisco, CA 94109, 415/776-2211).

- Read Colossians 1:9-14 aloud as your prayer. Thank God that Jesus has mended your broken relationship with nature, and ask him for love and wisdom to live out that reconciliation.

GLEANINGS
Keith Wright

Farms and orchards in your area may allow you to collect leftover fruit and vegetables for distribution to food ministries. Groups who have done this are often amazed at the amount of food they can collect in a day.

HABITAT FOR HUMANITY
Brian Hossink

Volunteer one Saturday or on a regular basis to help build homes with Habitat for Humanity (419 W. Church St., Americus, GA. 31709, 912/924-6135).

They can use people with a variety of skill levels—or no skills!

JOIN EVANGELICALS FOR SOCIAL ACTION

This organization, founded by Ron Sider, promotes peace and justice in public life. It has local chapters and a magazine *Prism*. Write to them at 10 Lancaster Ave., Philadelphia, PA 19151, or call 215/645-9390.

PROJECT WARMTH

Keith Wright

Collect blankets, coats and other warm clothing for the homeless. One group advertises their annual "blanket run" in the church newsletter and receives several truckloads of donated items. They also approach area businesses for monetary donations to buy rain ponchos and socks (the most requested items). Deliver your bounty to local homeless shelters and soup kitchens for distribution.

RACIAL RECONCILIATION

Brian Hossink

If your group is homogenous and you want to connect with people of other ethnicities, invite a Christian group or church of a different ethnic background to join you at your meetings. Attend their meetings. Cosponsor activities. This will allow you to build community and learn from one another.

SERVE THE HOMELESS

Brian Hossink

Go together to work at a local mission, shelter or soup kitchen. Get together and bake goods to send to a shelter or soup kitchen.

SPONSOR A CHILD

For a very small amount of money (perhaps $20 to $30 a month) your group can take care of the physical needs of a child in a developing country. The agency will send you pictures and information so that you can write the child and pray for him or her. Contact Compassion International, 12290

Voyager Parkway, Colorado Springs, CO 80921, or World Vision, 800 West Chestnut Avenue, Monrovia, CA 91016.

PRACTICE FRUGALITY

Find creative ideas for living more cheaply. The *Tightwad Gazette* books published by Villard Books are a great source of ideas. Talk about how you can live more economically in light of the needs of others and environmental stewardship. Make plans to give away the money you save.

VISIT NURSING HOMES

University of Illinois Staff

Prepare and share a worship service at a nursing home.

VOICELESS PEOPLE

Chuck Shelton

People without voices are powerless and cannot speak for themselves. Their needs go unmet and they suffer. They are the handicapped, the poor, abused women and children, the frail elderly, the unborn, the homeless, the hungry, the illiterate, the unemployed and people of color. To focus on the needs of the voiceless, read Isaiah 61:1-4. List ten actions to be taken by a person the Spirit of the Lord rests on. Beside each of these actions list an example of what living it out would look like in your community, church, family or campus. For example, working on a Habitat for Humanity project to build housing with the poor would "repair the ruined city." Select one of these actions and make plans to start doing it this week. (Adapted from *Voiceless People*, a Global Issues Bible Study [Downers Grove, Ill.: InterVarsity Press, 1990].)

WORLD AWARENESS WEEK

- Conduct studies on world hunger.
- Bring in speakers on specific topics like energy use.
- Encourage one another in lifestyle changes.

- Support Bread for the World (50 F Street, NW, Washington, D.C. 20001) or Food for the Hungry (7729 E. Greenway Road, Scottsdale, AZ 85260) or other groups that raise money to feed hungry people.

- Plan a hunger- or world-awareness meal for your church or fellowship.

- Use one day of the week for fasting and prayer for the world. (See section on Prayer Fast in chapter two.)

- Contact one of the following organizations for further ideas: Lutheran World Relief, 700 Light St., Baltimore, MD 21230, 410/230-2700; Mercy Corps International, 3030 SW First Avenue, Portland, OR 97201, 503/242-1032; World Concern, 19303 Fremont Ave. North, Seattle, WA 98133, 800/755-5022.

WRITE
Write letters to congressional representatives and other political officials on issues such as world hunger or energy.

BOOKS ON OUTREACH

Bakke, Raymond. *The Urban Christian*. Downers Grove, Ill.: InterVarsity Press, 1983. An excellent tool for those considering ministry in an urban setting. Bakke gives a brief theology of the city and tells of his own experiences and strategies.

Dawson, John. *Taking Our Cities for God*. Altamonte Springs, Fla.: Creation House, 1989. How we can pray for our cities.

Dearborn, Timothy. *Short-Term Missions Workbook*. Downers Grove, Ill.: InterVarsity Press, 2003. An eight-week preparation course for individuals and groups going on short-term mission trips.

Elmer, Duane. *Cross-Cultural Conflict*. Downers Grove, Ill.: InterVarsity Press, 1993. Each culture has a unique way of handling conflict; understanding the distinctives of cultural groups helps grow relationships. This book will introduce you to these dynamics.

Johnstone, Patrick. *Operation World*. 5th ed. Grand Rapids, Mich.: Zondervan, 1993. A daily guide to praying for the world, with facts about missions in every part of the world.

Knechtle, Cliffe. *Give Me an Answer*. Downers Grove, Ill.: InterVarsity Press, 1986. A seasoned evangelist gives answers to the questions seekers most frequently ask.

Little, Paul. *How to Give Away Your Faith*. Rev. ed. Downers Grove, Ill.: InterVarsity Press, 1988. Encouragement for those who are uncertain about how to share the gospel.

——. *Know Why You Believe*. Rev. ed. Downers Grove, Ill.: InterVarsity Press, 2000. Help in answering the hard questions you or others have about Christianity.

Malcolm, Kari Torjesen. *We Signed Away Our Lives*. Downers Grove, Ill.: InterVarsity Press, 1990. The story of a missionary family in China.

Perkins, Spencer, and Chris Rice. *More Than Equals*. Rev. ed. Downers Grove, Ill.: InterVarsity Press, 2000. Account of a friendship between a white man and an African American man that changed their perception of race relationships.

Pippert, Rebecca Manley. *Out of the Saltshaker*. 20th-anniversary ed.

Downers Grove, Ill.: InterVarsity Press, 1999. Classic call to evangelism by a former IVCF staffworker with many motivating and inspiring stories.

Richardson, Rick. *Evangelism Outside the Box.* Downers Grove, Ill.: InterVarsity Press, 2000. Issues in bringing the gospel to a postmodern generation.

Sider, Ronald J. *Rich Christians in an Age of Hunger.* Waco, Tex.: Word, 1990. A challenge to use material resources well in light of the needs of those around you and of the whole world.

Stiles, J. Mack. *Speaking of Jesus.* Downers Grove, Ill.: InterVarsity Press, 1995. An inspiring and practical book on sharing the gospel with friends.

Teter, John. *Get the Word Out.* Downers Grove, Ill.: InterVarsity Press, 2003. A fresh look at how God goes before us and follows after us in our evangelistic efforts.

BIBLE STUDIES ON OUTREACH

Borthwick, Paul. *Missions.* A LifeGuide® Bible Study. Downers Grove, Ill.: InterVarsity Press, 2000. 9 studies on God's heart for the gospel to spread throughout the world.

Richardson, Rick. Groups Investigating God Series. Downers Grove, Ill.: InterVarsity Press, 2002. Bible study guides for use with seekers. Six sessions in each guide.

Scazzero, Peter. *Introducing Jesus.* Downers Grove, Ill.: InterVarsity Press, 1991. A brief book that explains how to start an investigative Bible discussion group for seekers. Six Bible studies that can be photocopied for the group are included.

Sire, James. *Jesus the Reason.* A LifeGuide® Bible Study. Downers Grove, Ill.: InterVarsity Press, 1996. Eleven studies on who Jesus is and why he is the basis of our faith. Great for seekers.

INCORPORATING CHILDREN AND YOUTH

Here are some different ideas about various ways to care for the children of small group members. There are different levels of involvement. "Baby-Sitting Options" explores ways to arrange child-care. "Evaluating the Options" is a survey you can use as to start discussing how to handle child-care in your group. "Intergenerational Small Groups" talks about how to incorporate children into the group. "How to Have a Children's Group" provides an outline for a children's small group time as part of a larger adult group.

BABY-SITTING OPTIONS

Michael C. Mack

Here are some ideas from a Christianity Today message board discussion for ways to handle baby-sitting during small group.

1. Parents pay for baby-sitting in their own homes. (Perhaps several parents who live nearby can go together.)

2. Group members pool together for a babysitter at another home.

3. Older children or youth care for the younger children in the same home as the meeting or in another home.

4. Children are part of the group. (This has worked in a number of churches, but it takes lots of planning and patience.)

Another respondent said group members in his church provide childcare for one another on a rotating basis. He says this promotes four things:

1. Each adult has the opportunity to transfer biblical values from his or her own perspective to the children. In other words, my kids benefit from your relationship with Jesus.

2. It promotes more of a sense of community among group members.

3. Adults have the chance to see the faith and faithfulness of the children, and are therefore encouraged by them.

4. It promotes the idea that children are important in the life of the church.

Having each adult who cares for children fill out a confidential information form is recommended. Only after the references are checked can the adults work with the children. This measure protects the church, children, parents and children's workers.

Here are a couple other ideas I've come across.

1. Work with the youth minister to set up something with some of the teens of the church to provide child-care. This is not a "ministry" for the teenagers; they should be paid for their time.

2. Ask grandparents in the church whose grandchildren live far away to

play with and care for the children, perhaps in return for chores done around their houses by the group.

Remember that each group is different and thus has different needs, especially in relation to the age of the kids. Ultimately, child-care decisions ought to be up to each group, but church leaders should be available to coordinate and problem solve.

One more thing to consider. child-care workers need training and support. We should not just dump the kids in the hands of an untrained person who has no plan for working with the children. Materials need to be provided for the kids to learn at their own level. Look for resources that go along with what the parents are studying or find some quality Christian videos to use.

Small groups can be a great opportunity for the children to learn and grow as well as the adults. Since the kids see each other nearly every week, some of their best friendships may blossom in the group.

EVALUATING THE OPTIONS
Michael C. Mack

Take this quiz to help you decide about child-care options. Every church's small group ministry—and each group—is different, so there are no right or wrong answers. But you can think through the choices that will work best in your situation. Child-care can be a great opportunity rather than a burden, if you plan.

____1. What is the policy for your group? (a) no children except for nursing infants (b) intergenerational—we include all children (c) take turns caring for the children (d) hire a baby-sitter for the whole group (e) another option

____2. Where should child-care be provided? (a) in the same house as the Bible study, but in a separate room as far from the meeting as possible (b) at the baby-sitter's house (c) at the church building (d) wherever individual parents want it to be

___3. Who pays for child-care? (a) the parents (b) the group passes around a hat (c) no one—it's free (d) the church treasury (e) the group leader

___4. What training will be supplied for child-care providers? (a) basic safety instructions (b) how to handle discipline (c) how to engage children in involvement learning and interactive play (d) a basic understanding of age levels (e) diaper changing (f) all of the above (g) none of the above—all they have to do is watch the kids

___5. What resources will be provided for child-care? (a) Christian videos, such as McGee and Me (b) reading books for different age groups (c) games and puzzles (d) coloring and activity books (e) teacher's helps (f) several of the above

___6. What groups or individuals do you use for child-care? (a) the youth group—the youth minister recruits teens to minister in this way, and they make some extra spending money too (b) "grandparents"—older members of the church, especially those who don't have grandkids or those whose grandchildren live far away (c) rotating people in the groups (d) members of other groups who meet other nights of the week—and we return the favor (e) Mr. Rogers

___7. Who is responsible for finding and training child-care workers, as well as for providing resources and following up with workers? (a) each small group leader (b) a designated person in each group, possibly the apprentice (c) the small groups administrator (coach) (d) the CE director (e) the youth minister (f) all or some of the above work together

___8. What are the children taught? (a) it depends—children play and child-care workers interact with them, looking for teachable moments (b) applications based on Sunday school lessons (c) lessons that go along with parents' Bible study—gives family opportunity to discuss study together later (d) program developed for this situation (e) nothing in particular

HOW TO HAVE A CHILDREN'S GROUP
Holly Allen

What is a children's small group? It is a small group of children bonded together around a leader for mutual care, prayer, questioning and discussion. Living their Christian life together, they reach out to serve others and to win other children to follow Jesus. This small group is a subgroup of the family group. The goal of children's groups is to meet children's spiritual needs much as adult groups meet adults' spiritual needs.

When I asked some of the children in a small group what their special memories of children's small group time were, they said:

- 7-year-old: "I remember when Mr. Leonard (senior pastor) sat on the floor with us and listened to us."

- 4-year-old: "I like to be with the big kids and do what they do. They let me talk and everything."

- 15-year-old: "I remember when Jeff blindfolded us and led us around the furniture. He said that is the way God leads us, and we should trust him."

- 9-year-old: "I remember when I was afraid to go to public school because I had been home-schooled. All the kids prayed for me."

To facilitate the children's group, each small group should designate a children's small group coordinator. This person does not lead every children's meeting, but he or she gives oversight to the ministry to the children. Each week adult small group members take turns as the children's group leader. Everyone in the group should be able to love the children and lead them through simple activities and stories.

What do you do in the children's small group? The common components include an icebreaker, prayer, Bible story, theme activities, sharing struggles and victories, listening, and regrouping with the adults.

Icebreaker

The icebreaker is usually a simple, nonthreatening question like, "What is your favorite ice cream?" Sometimes the question connects to the Bible story or biblical theme being emphasized that evening, such as, "What would be difficult about being raised in a king's palace?" (This icebreaker accompanies the story about Moses being raised in Pharaoh's house.)

Each child usually answers the icebreaker, though it is not "required." Visitors are encouraged to answer but are given an easy "out" by saying, "Would you like to tell us your favorite zoo animal or would you like to pass?"

The children look forward to the icebreaker each week and expect it. Though the icebreaker time is light and easy, it can lead to deeper discussions and prayer. I remember when the story time was about Ananias and Sapphira, and the icebreaker was "Can you think of a time when you told a lie and got caught?" I began the icebreaker by confessing a lie I told to my sixth grade teacher and how he found out and what happened to me.

The children were fascinated by my story and wanted to hear all the details and how it turned out. Two or three remembered specific lies (and consequences). A preschooler said there were monsters under his bed. One second grader said that she sometimes didn't tell the truth, and she was afraid that she was a really bad person. We prayed with her for forgiveness.

In this case, the icebreaker led to confession and a way to acknowledge and work through the sin and the fear.

Prayer

This is a time for sharing victories and struggles. The children's small group coordinator keeps the prayer journal that is passed each week to the children's group leader so that last week's prayer needs can be reviewed.

One week a tender-hearted child (Erin) asked the group to pray for a girl at her school who was being bullied (Sara). The next week the other children asked how the week had gone for Sara. "Not very well," was the response. Another child suggested they pray for the main bully (Justin). They did. Every week for months the children prayed for Sara and Justin. Eventually Erin asked that they pray for her. She wanted to befriend Sara, not just pray for her. A few weeks later Erin asked that they pray that she might publicly defend Sara. Each week the current group leader noticed the prayer need in the journal, and each week the children prayed. Though

Justin was still bullying Sara at the end of the school year, the whole children's group realized the biggest change happened in Erin. She had learned to stand up with courage for a friend.

Bible Story

The children's group should also include a Bible story told in an active way. For example, the children pass around a heavy rock while the teacher tells the story of the Israelites as slaves in Egypt from Exodus 1. Or you can develop a thumbs-up, thumbs-down script.

- The spies went into the land as God had told them. (thumbs up)
- Ten spies said the land was too hard to take. (thumbs down)
- Two spies said the Lord would enable the Israelites to win. (thumbs up)
- The Israelites believed the ten spies. (thumbs down)

A more active way is for the children to stand up or sit down instead of using their thumbs. The children's group leader can decide how active the storytelling needs to be.

There are a variety of creative ways to communicate the Bible stories. Sometimes a script for adult "actors" (parents or other adult group members) is included. Other times the children are given art supplies to draw the story as it is told. Sometimes directions are given for helping the children enact the story. The goal is not only to communicate facts but also to provide an opportunity for children to learn by interacting with adults and one another.

Share Personal Insights

At this point, the children's group leader is encouraged to share a time when God has worked powerfully in her own life. This is the time when the most significant things happen in the children's small group. When the various adults who take turns leading the children's group share what God has been doing in their lives, confess areas of weakness and pray for God's guidance, the children see God is working in the Christians around them. They discover that the adults they know seek God in all they do. Basically, the children are privy to the "normal Christian life" as lived by the adults in their church.

Sometimes following the sharing, there is a time for "listening" to God, a time for making Scripture real and usable, or a time for asking for God's empowerment in overcoming sin or for healing.

Regrouping with Adults

When group time is over, the children regroup with the adults for a few minutes to share something they did in their group time. They might repeat the "thumbs up, thumbs down" activity, reenact the story or share food they have made. They might say the Ten Commandments or a memory verse or share an answered prayer. This closure activity signals to the adults that the children's group is over, therefore the adult group needs to end soon. Also, the children get to share what they have been doing, helping them (and their parents) realize that these activities are important, not merely busywork.

Just like adults, children need a place to be accepted and loved, to share their needs and fears, to pray for others and to be prayed for, to forgive, to confess, to experience God. A children's small group can be that place.

INTERGENERATIONAL SMALL GROUPS
Janet Busboom

Child: "May I come to your cell today. To see you worship, sing and pray?"

Adult   "You wouldn't find it any fun. When you are older, you may come." ("The Unwelcome Child" by Lorna Jenkins)

Sadly, most of us have looked at children in small groups the same way this poem does: as a logistical nightmare. But it doesn't have to be that way. Although parents have the primary responsibility of nurturing, discipling and equipping their children, we recognize the church body is the extended spiritual family of every child.

Every child can live a full Christian life. They are capable of praying effectively, worshiping in Spirit and truth, and are able to receive the Holy

Spirit and operate in his gifts. They should be equipped to witness, serve and model Christ to those around them.

An intergenerational small group functions like any other small group or cell group—except there are children in the group. These children are considered to be full and active members. Their needs and desires are to be taken into account with those of the adults in planning the group meetings. The leader helps children actively participate and, in some cases, lead in the icebreaker, worship, prayer time and Communion.

Most children will not sit through a discussion that centers around adult needs. Therefore, it is likely that a children's small group time should be developed to take place during the Bible study portion of the meeting.

If you don't currently incorporate children in your small group, bring it up as a matter of discussion, and see what new opportunities the conversation opens up.

BUILDING BRIDGES TO ETHNIC MINORITIES

Greg Jao, Allen Wakabayashi, Beth Hedges and Sandra Van Opstal

We often assume that others are a lot like us. Therefore, we relate to them in ways that we find most comfortable, and we expect them to relate to us in ways we are most accustomed to. Here are some ideas for crossethnic communication to help people of diverse backgrounds feel comfortable in your small group.

BUILDING BRIDGES TO ASIAN AMERICANS

While language barriers are not at issue when relating to Asian Americans, there are subtle cultural issues that may be at play as they interact with you. If these differences are not taken into account, you may unwittingly miss opportunities to connect deeply with them. These tips, while not comprehensive, suggest what may be going on in Asian American group members and how you can more effectively engage them.

Recognize Asian Cultural Relational Values

- *Hierarchy.* You may notice Asian Americans may be less participatory and assertive. Asian culture inculcates a strong sense of hierarchy and position. They will likely look to you, as an older leader, to take initiative in conversation and interaction.

- *Harmony.* Asian cultures value a high sensitivity to the community and its relational harmony. For example, many Asian Americans feel that blurting out how they feel or what they think is selfish. It forces the group (and the group leader) not only to bear the weight of—but also to respond to—what is shared by the individual. (In their mind, this may distract people from the concerns of the group as a whole). To assert oneself in any way is felt to be self-serving and disrespectful to others. Therefore, some of the best contributions to a discussion may be lost because a leader does not know how to draw out Asian Americans.

- *Humility.* If a question requires sharing one's strengths or achievements, Asian Americans may be reticent to speak because, in a traditional Asian context, this kind of sharing would be considered arrogant boasting. (It requires the individual to rank oneself above the group. This differs from Western values that encourage individual self-assertion.) Therefore, taking a leadership role or strongly asserting one's opinion is very difficult to do in light of the Asian sensitivity to relational harmony.

Recognize They Are Bicultural

Asian American have both Western and Asian values swirling beneath the surface. Therefore, not every Asian American will express all these values.

Some Asian Americans have caught the message that it is best to assimilate into the dominant culture; therefore, they have learned how to be assertive and highly verbal. Others are aware of the Asian values tucked away deep inside; therefore, they have learned to step out of those values in a mixed ethnic setting. Most Asian Americans, however, are not very aware of these cultural realities. They will be quiet, unassuming and very compliant while not knowing why they are that way and how deep-seated Asian values engender those kinds of relational characteristics. That is why a lot of these explanations are stated in terms of how the Asian American is "feeling" rather than what they are thinking. Most of the dynamics that Asian Americans exhibit operate at a preconscious level that is deep-seated and, for most, preverbal: that is, they can't even articulate themselves why they are feeling and acting the way that they do.

Suggestions

- *Take initiative.* If they are wrestling with issues, it will be very hard for many Asian Americans to take initiative with you or to share very freely with the small group. Take seriously your role and position as a small group leader in their life. They expect you to take initiative if you want to know what is going on. Take time one-on-one outside of small group to ask. By your taking initiative, they will be freer to share what is going on inside.

- *Entrusting leadership or contribution.* The key to drawing out an Asian American is *entrustment.* If an Asian American is entrusted by the leader with the responsibility for leading or contributing something, then that Asian American has been freed up to do so without fear of appearing self-serving or disrespectful. So, for instance, if you hear something from an Asian American that you wish others in your small group could hear, then entrust that Asian American with the responsibility of sharing it: "John, that's a wonderful testimony of God's work! Why don't you share that with the group next time we meet?" Then at the group meeting, as the leader, invite their contribution: "John told me something wonderful this afternoon. John, why don't you tell the group what you told me?"

This frees up John to be open and contribute to the group without appearing to be motivated by a desire to draw attention to himself.

• *Appropriate naming.* In general, avoid putting someone on the spot by calling on them by name to answer more personal questions like "How are you going to apply this to your life?" or "How is God calling you to change your life in response to this session?" However, when the subject matter does not require a high degree of vulnerability, it is sometimes appropriate to call on the quieter Asian American by name for a response. For instance, the question, "What did you think of what the speaker said about . . . ?" is not a threatening question.

• *Be aware of volume and proximity.* Without realizing it, we have a norm for the volume level with which we speak and for how closely you stand to the person you are speaking to. For the Asian American, volume tends to be notch lower (quieter) than for the Caucasian, African American and Latino. And the physical distance in conversation tends to be just a tad bit farther away than what is typical for the non-Asian. This is rather hard to judge, but be sensitive so that you don't back your Asian American to the wall by how close you are standing or how loudly you are speaking.

• *Don't tell the Asian American, "I'm doing this because you're Asian."* Most will not appreciate hearing that at all. Simply be aware of the dynamics and relate accordingly.

BUILDING BRIDGES TO AFRICAN AMERICANS

Blacks are a diverse community in our society. Some are African Americans with a long history of slavery and oppression going back over ten generations. This long history affects their relationship with the dominant culture. However the black community also includes Caribbean Americans and more recent African immigrants such as Nigerians. These more recent immigrants have a different relationship with the majority American culture and even with African American culture. Despite these different cultural backgrounds, all blacks are caught in our racially divided society. The racial assumptions commonly made in employment, policing, housing and other areas have an impact on all of them.

Recognize That Black History and Experience Influence Everything

Blacks, as a discriminated-against minority, have learned to be careful about letting outsiders in. It is not unusual for blacks to be cautious in relationships because in the past they have been hurt by those who do not understand that their everyday experience is very different than what the mainstream media and culture assume to be true. Over the course of a conference there is not a lot of time to build trust to overcome this reticence.

Recognize African American Cultural/Relational Values

- *Communication.* The African American community values being direct in communication. Those who speak the truth are respected, and confrontation is often embraced.

- *Authority:* In the African American church, those who have been given power in the church are highly respected. One needs to show respect toward pastors and other leaders in the church, and there is often a certain level of formality in this relationship. As a small group leader you will fall, in some ways, into this category.

- *Expression:* African American culture is exuberant, which can be seen in music, dance, conversation and physical interaction.

Suggestions

- *Acknowledge different experiences.* Don't assume that everyone's experience of majority culture is the same. Welcome disagreement and other perspectives on reality. When you are giving examples or illustrations, acknowledge that they are specific to you and to your cultural and family experience, not an experience that all have or even a typically "American" experience.

- *Expect that communication will be complex.* As an authority you will have respect, but trust in the relationship will take a lot longer. Being authentic and keeping it real will help trust grow.

- *Be sensitive to culture shock.* The focus in the black church is exhortation and preaching, not small group discussion. So interactive learning may be a very new concept for your group members.

- *Demonstrate vulnerability.* In white culture you show interest in someone by asking lots of questions. For blacks this can feel like an inquisition, which causes them to feel exposed and vulnerable. Be vulnerable first.

- *Learning together.* The black church has a long tradition of bringing the gospel to bear on societal problems. This perspective deepens Bible study and scriptural application so that it reflects the values of the kingdom. Think about how what is being learned can apply to issues like racism, oppression and injustice in politics and economics. Being an advocate for these issues with your small group is one powerful way to care for blacks.

BUILDING BRIDGES TO LATINOS

Within the diversity of the Latino community, there are a few things to keep in mind as you try to engage them.

Recognize Latino Cultural/Relational Values

- *Honesty.* Latinos have a way of being up-front about their opinions. They like to process in groups and therefore will probably be engaged in the group dialogue. It would not be uncommon to have a Latino person be extremely direct in sharing their thoughts. They also like to challenge the opinions of others, so if someone in your group has expressed an idea and they do not agree, it is likely they will say "I don't agree because . . ." This honesty is normal and highly valued in the Latino context but can sometimes be seen as argumentative. They are also very perceptive in whether or not someone is being honest, and they are put off by those who are not. They may even call you on it!

- *Expression.* Latinos highly value the freedom to express themselves, verbally as well as physically. Coming from a culture characterized by storytelling, they will enjoy a small group that accepts liveliness in the sharing time. When given the space, they might respond to another member of the group with a word of encouragement, a hug or other signs of affirmation. This is a way of expressing that inside they are in agreement.

Recognize That "Latinos" Consist of Many Ethnicities and Cultures

It is important to note that the Latino experience is extremely different for each culture. For example, *Latino* can be used to describe a fourth-generation, English-speaking biracial Puerto Rican from the inner city of Chicago or a second-generation, bilingual white Argentine from an upper-middle-class suburb. Obviously the experiences that these two people have had and they way they approach being in a small group of people who are from majority culture will be different. Be aware that because of their experiences they may or may not have difficulty trusting you as their leader or the rest of the group members.

As Latinos in America they are also bicultural, so they will exhibit signs of having both North American and Latino American values. For example, although family plays such a crucial role in decision making, you may have someone in your group who speaks in a way that sounds very independent and individualistic. This person cares about what their family thinks, but the American value of freedom and individual choice makes more sense to them. They have two sets of values that conflict in some areas and are in harmony in others, so they will have to choose.

Suggestions

- *Don't be surprised by anything they say.* Latinos tend to be unpredictable in the way they respond to questions or comments. But if they have an opinion, it will probably come with some energy behind it. Try to stay neutral; let them know in some way that they have been heard.

- *Ask questions, affirm them and challenge them.* If you have the opportunity to speak with the Latinos in your group one on one, take that opportunity to ask them if they are enjoying the track or small group. Engage them in dialogue on what you are learning. If you feel like you understand where they are coming from, feel free to affirm them and challenge them. They will respect you for your honesty and welcome a lively discussion.

- *Keep in mind that a large majority of Christian Latinos are Catholic.* Although you should not assume that everyone is, it is safe to say that it is likely. Reflect on your own attitudes toward Catholicism and any biases you may inadvertently express.

PERMISSIONS

The following ideas are used by permission of the Small Group Network.

Community
Community Evaluation, Mike Mack

Worship & Prayer
Fill in the Blank (from *12 Ideas for Conversational Prayer*)
Keep a Prayer Diary (from *12 Ideas for Conversational Prayer*)
Keep It Short (from *12 Ideas for Conversational Prayer*)
Lead Worship, Dan Smith and Steven Reames
Make It Personal (from *12 Ideas for Conversational Prayer*)
Pick a Prayer (from *12 Ideas for Conversational Prayer*)
Pray in One Voice (from *12 Ideas for Conversational Prayer*)
Pray the Night Away, Keith D. Wright
Study Prayer (from *12 Ideas for Conversational Prayer*)

Study
Application Questions for Bible Study, Mike Shepherd
Assign Homework, Jeff Grant
Help People Learn, Mike Shepherd
Integrate Your Icebreaker, Dan Lentz
Make Bible Study More Interactive, James M. Kovach
Portfolio of Promises, Keith D. Wright
Selections from *Jesus the Group Leader, Part 5*, Mike Shepherd
Set the Bar for Great Bible Discussion, Mike Shepherd

Outreach
Emphasize Service, Murphy Belding
Take Your Small Group to the People, Dan Lentz
Various Ways to Serve Your Community, Keith D. Wright

Appendix A: Incorporating Children and Youth
Adventures in Baby-Sitting, Michael C. Mack
Children Love Small Groups! Holly Allen
Intergenerational Cell Groups, Janet Busboom

THE SMALL GROUP NETWORK
www.SmallGroups.com

The Small Group Network is an Internet-based ministry providing training and resources for Christian small groups. Individuals, churches, publishers and other Christian organizations work together to support small group leaders and administrators of groups in making disciples—and making disciples into disciplemakers.

SmallGroups.com is a resource for those involved in any facet of small group ministry:

- pastors and preachers
- administrators of small group ministries
- leaders and facilitators of groups
- apprentices, assistant leaders, interns, coleaders
- small group coaches
- hosts and hostesses
- people interested in being involved in small groups
- people involved in recovery and support groups, discipleship groups, accountability groups, care groups, adult fellowship groups, Sunday school classes and any other type of Christian group

For more information on the Small Group Network or to view more resources, contact: **Small Group Network**

P.O. Box 621
Zionsville, IN 46077
317-769-0945
office@smallgroups.com
www.SmallGroups.com